Collecting for Tomorrow

SPOONS

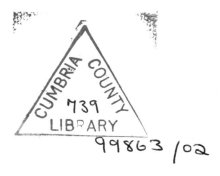

This series is written by experts and specially designed for the collector who is interested in modestly priced and readily available items of the 19th and 20th centuries.

Other titles available in the series:

Kitchenware by Jo Marshall
Candlesticks by Deborah Stratton
Boxes by Brian Cole

Collecting for Tomorrow

SPOONS

MICHAEL SNODIN
AND
GAIL BELDEN

Pitman Publishing

First published in Great Britain in 1976
by Pitman Publishing Ltd
39 Parker Street, London WC2B 5PB

© Walter Parrish International Limited 1976

Designed and produced by
Walter Parrish International Ltd., London

Made and printed in Great Britain by
Purnell and Sons Limited,
Paulton near Bristol, Avon, England

ISBN 0 273 00236 8
G50:14

Contents

Introduction

Styles

The spoon was one of the earliest utensils to be fashioned by man, and as a group they offer a wide and extremely varied field to the collector. Most of the spoons seen today in antique shops and even in many kitchen drawers date from the 19th century, a period during which there was a sudden increase in the production of metal spoons in a vast and bewildering range of sizes, types and styles. This surge of activity was the direct result of new mechanized methods and materials. Until then, the form of the modern spoon had developed along a steady line, its general shape characterized by a straight, flat handle or stem which, when seen from the side, is more or less in line with the (usually oval) hollowed portion or bowl. The earliest spoon of this type was the French 'trifid' of the mid-17th century. Subsequent developments in England were the Hanoverian and Old English patterns.

Eighteenth-century America tended to follow the English lead but developments on the Continent of Europe were different, and greatly influenced by France. The fiddle pattern with its stem spreading at the end, had appeared in France by 1700, and by the mid-18th century most of the well-known variations with shell decorations and moulded or threaded edges were being made in France and other Continental countries.

The complex relief decoration on these spoons was stamped with engraved steel dies, a technique that soon led, in France, to the stamping of complete spoons and the production of the first standardized patterns, which facilitated and encouraged the making of comprehensive, matching services.

The idea of matching spoons, knives and forks, known collectively as flatware, began in the late 17th century at which time the different sizes of table and dessert spoons also emerged. Services were not common until the late 18th century. By the late 19th century, they had become very elaborate, and incorporated many of the specialized implements, spoons and ladles which had evolved since the mid-18th century. Services have been considerably simplified since. Pieces of flatware had been growing steadily bigger since the mid-18th century and by 1800, they had become very large. From about 1870 onwards, however, flatware tended to decrease in size.

The fiddle pattern dominated flatware in the 19th century and, in its plain version, it was made in slightly different forms all over Europe and America. The pattern was also very popular when decorated with die stamped relief ornament, which ranged from the restrained classicism of the King's pattern to vigorous adaptations of 18th-century rococo and of so-called 'Gothic' and 'Tudor' ornament.

After about 1900, the fiddle pattern lost favour in response to an international revival of French designs of the late 18th century and the Empire. This tended to produce weak variants of the original patterns. The revivals were frequently mixed with elements drawn from the new decorative art styles, Art Nouveau and Jugendstil.

Historicism, or the imitation of past styles, was vitally important in the art of the 19th century, and it had a considerable influence on spoons which were made outside the range of standard patterns, such as dessert services, condiment spoons, teaspoons and other specialized types. Pieces evoking the Renaissance and the Middle Ages had a particularly strong appeal, their delicate, elaborately shaped stems and finials providing a welcome contrast to the large, massively modelled fiddle pattern types.

In the 1940s and 1950s, there was a general turning away from older designs and towards modern functional forms. Many 19th-century patterns, however, continued to be made.

Materials, Manufacture and Marketing

Nineteenth-century spoonmaking is remarkable for the wide range of metals and plating processes employed as cheap substitutes for silver. Of the twenty-eight spoonmakers listed in a Birmingham directory of 1818, ten made spoons of tinned iron, five used Tutania, an alloy of brass, antimony and tin, and two, Britannia-metal. Britannia-metal, with slight variations in the alloys, also appeared under a number of different names, such as 'Crown Metal' which was used by Yates of Birmingham, and 'Queen's Metal', by Ashberry of Sheffield.

From the 1830s onwards, spoons were made of German or nickel silver, a nickel alloy with a yellowish sheen somewhat resembling silver in appearance. Initially, and briefly, it was close-plated with silver, but after 1840, it became the universal standard base metal for electro-deposited silver. It continued to be used unplated in England, where it was generally called British Plate and stamped 'BP'. Nickel silver in its differing alloys was known by a variety of names, including Argentan (an original German name), Argentine (a term used by the 1830s in England), Alfenide (invented by the French chemist Halphen, in 1851), *Neusilber,* Alpaka and Alpacca (used both in Scandinavia and Germany) as well as by many names with South American silver-mining connections, such as 'Potosi Silver'.

The process of coating nickel with pure silver by electro-deposition was patented by the Birmingham firm of Elkington Mason and Company in 1840 and EPNS (electroplated nickel silver) soon caused a revolution in flatware manufacture. The plating was available in different thicknesses and in England was loosely graded A, B, and C, the last described in a Dixon of Sheffield catalogue as 'cheaply got up and suitable for exportation'. Christofle, the principal French electroplating firm, introduced a system, also taken up by other French manufacturers, of indicating the weight of silver deposited; '84' on a tablespoon, for instance, indicates 84 grams of silver per dozen spoons.

An indication of comparative prices in 1907 is given by the London Army and Navy Stores for tablespoons per dozen in different metals: silver, £5 14s 0d; EPNS, £1 7s 0d; unplated nickel silver, 10s 0d; aluminium, 2s 7d; tinned iron, 1s 7d. A catalogue of about 1882 of the London suppliers, Silber & Fleming, lists 'corrugated tinned iron . . . tablespoons' at 9s a gross, and Britannia-metal tablespoons from 19s 6d and £1 5s 9d (steel wire lined) a gross. Also listed are egg, mustard, salt and marrow spoons of bone. The Christofle catalogue of 1898 includes not only models for the French taste, but also contains eight pages of patterns suitable for export to Spain, Italy, Poland, Eastern Europe, Holland and Great Britain. Manufacturers in other countries also catered for foreign markets.

The traditional spoonmaking materials, wood, bone and horn, had fallen out of general use by 1900, but survived for specialized uses, notably in medicine, for which spoons were also made in earthenware, porcelain, cut glass, ivory and pewter.

Marks and Hall-marks

The practice of hall-marking in England (named after the Hall of the London Goldsmiths' Company) was instituted in the 14th century to guarantee the maintenance of the silver standard, which in Britain is 925 (sterling standard) or 958 (Britannia standard) parts of pure silver in 1000 parts of alloyed metal. (Silver must be alloyed, mainly with copper, to strengthen it.) British 19th-century sterling silver made up to 1890 should have five marks: the duty mark (the monarch's head, introduced in 1784 and deleted in 1890); the lion passant mark (often called the 'sterling mark'); the town mark (in London, a leopard's head); the date letter, and the maker's mark. The 'maker's mark', however, is frequently the mark of the retailing firm and is more correctly described in the British Hall-Marking Act of 1973 as the 'sponsor's mark'. Small British spoons made before about 1780 often bear only the maker's mark and the lion passant.

Silver standards in the rest of Europe, with the exception of France, were, and remain, generally lower than sterling. They often hover at about 800 parts of silver to 1000, and in the late 19th century most countries adopted systems in which the silver content is indicated by numerals. German spoons, for instance, after 1888, when the mark of a crown and crescent was introduced to indicate standard, frequently carry the numeral '800'. Before that date Germany and Scandinavia used to mark by 'lot', dividing a weight measure into 16 lots, the full 16 meaning pure silver. Thus, lot marks of '13' and '12', commonly found on their spoons, indicate respectively alloys of 812 and 750 parts of silver. The Russians, employing a similar system, divided their standard weight into 96 'zolotniks', 96 meaning pure silver. The '84' therefore which is often stamped on their products, means 875/1000.

English electroplate manufacturers, following a practice begun by close-platers, imitated hall-marks both in the size and placing of their marks. The marks frequently read EPNS, and many firms also used identifying devices, trade names such as 'Potosi Silver' and quality marks. Elkington's employed a letter system to denote the year of manufacture, details of which have survived. French electroplate marks closely imitate their silver counterparts and often read *'métal blanc'* and include numerals indicating the weight of the silver deposited. Christofle also used a system of date numbers, '94' standing for 1894. The Alpacca and *'Neusilber'* of Germany and Scandinavia are frequently stamped 'Alp' or 'NS'.

British spoons in all materials between 1842 and 1883 can also bear a diamond-shaped registered design mark. After that, a series of numbers, which is still in use, was instituted for each item registered at the Patent Office by the designer or manufacturer. These were protected from imitation for three years from the date of registration of the mark. A key to dating the marks is given by Shirley Bury and Patricia Wardle (*see* Bibliography). Details of marks, registration numbers and the registering firms prior to 1910 can be traced at the Public Records Office, London. Records since that date are held by the Patent Office. In the United States, designs could be similarly patented.

Hints to Collectors

Spoons dating from after 1800 are on the whole still too low in price to tempt the faker, but contemporary copies of English spoons were made in China in the 19th century. Rather clumsily shaped versions of simple English patterns, they bear false hall-marks, as well as fairly good copies of marks of contemporary London silversmiths, such as the WE/WF/WC of the notable spoonmakers, Eley, Fearn and Chawner, who worked from 1808 to 1814. Marks used in Canada, the United States and India in the same period also imitated English and Scottish marks, but cannot be called fakes.

Certain types of 19th-century spoons have now become expensive, such as those made by Paul Storr and pre-revolutionary Russian enamel spoons. There remains, however, a vast and reasonably priced field open to the collector. Britannia-metal and iron spoons, once so common and now quite rare, are beginning to attract a following. So also are some very attractive and relatively short-lived English patterns made in silver and electroplate in the mid-19th century. These materials were used for many of the elegant and desirable spoons produced by the Art Nouveau, Jugendstil and Arts and Crafts movements from about 1890 to 1910. Modern spoon patterns based on functional principles seem to go out of fashion almost as quickly as earlier patterns did and are already being collected by museums.

In America, both English and American spoons are available, with pre-1850 English spoons in particularly good supply. 18th-century examples will be found only in the finest antique shops, but 19th-century tea, table, soup, dessert, and serving spoons plus a fair number of large and small ladles will be available next to an array of salt, mustard, ice-cream, and egg spoons, sugar sifters, and pickle scoops.

The wise collector should look for well-made and designed spoons, and always buy the best quality he can afford. If he likes rarities he should study patterns and their frequency of manufacture, and learn the names of firms, their output, working dates, and locations. Or he will carry a very large book. If he wants to collect every pattern of one firm or an example from every firm in a certain city, or a dozen matching examples of each form, he will learn the firm's output, the city's manufacturers, and the shapes and uses of specialized forms.

His finds will be usable, unbreakable, easily carried, and easily stored; they will please the eye, and above all, they will evoke the tastes and customs of a past age.

NOTE.
All the spoons in this book are silver, unless otherwise indicated.

Early metals: pewter, Britannia

To find a hundred-year-old pewter spoon is difficult. Pewter's composition of tin and lead with a little antimony and bismuth resulted in a soft metal that wore down rapidly and broke with repeated bending, causing housewives to turn it back to the pewterer for the melting pot.

Discovering a spoon of Britannia-metal is easier. Britannia was an alloy similar to pewter, which consisted of three parts copper and ten parts antimony added to 150 parts tin; the lead was all but omitted to produce a more durable ware. It was promoted by James Vickers of Sheffield, who bought the formula in 1769 from its creator, M. Gower, and by 1787 was making Britannia measures, pots, caster-frames and salt spoons. William Will, a Philadelphia pewterer, owned the formula in 1799, and by 1825 Ashbel Griswold was using it in Meriden, Connecticut.

Both pewter and Britannia could be cast, rolled, hammered, spun or pressed. In the 18th century, pewter spoons were made by pouring molten metal into iron or bronze moulds; in the 19th, pewter and Britannia spoons were made by pressing sheet metal between two dies. They were both finished by a rubbing with rotten-stone and oil and were kept shiny by the owner with a polish of whiting.

Britannia spoons were sold side by side with silver and gold objects by men who listed themselves in American city directories as silversmiths, spoonmakers or dealers in watches and jewellery, or as manufacturers, importers, fancy-goods or dry-goods dealers and repairers of watches, clocks and jewellery.

Teaspoon, pewter, 1787-1811; an extremely rare example; rounded, downturned, feather-edged handle, drop on bowl back; impressed decoration of crossed American flags flanking a liberty cap on a pole above a banner bearing 'Peace with Amity', above a bowknot with leafy pendants; maker's mark: G. COLDWELL in serrated rectangle (George Coldwell, New York, New York); $8\frac{7}{16}$ inches.

Iron, brass and Sheffield plate

Cheap spoons of pewter and brass were made in imitation of silver spoons in late medieval times. The brass was often tinned to look more convincing, and the pewter, of course, was originally bright. Such brass spoons were still produced in the 18th century, but by the century's end appear to have been replaced by iron spoons, tinned or close-plated, which became standard kitchen equipment. Though once extremely common, surviving examples are rare. The spoon shown here is a finely-shaped example, either cast or wrought, but they were also simply stamped out of thin sheets of metal.

Pewter spoons in general were outmoded, starting in the late 18th century, by those of Britannia-metal. Sheffield plating, traditionally invented in 1743, is a process by which silver is fused onto a copper base, and when rolled into sheets or drawn into wire, is capable of being worked like silver. Sheffield flatware, although cheaper than silver, proved complicated to make and not very durable; consequently, it was produced briefly, only towards the end of the 18th century. Stems of spoons were rolled out of plated wire, and bowls had to be made separately. The stem of the ladle shown here is made of two stamped-out halves soldered together, to which the bowl has been attached; the edge of the bowl is protected against wear by a wire of solid silver. The gilded copper egg spoon, although it is not silver-plated, is nevertheless by a Sheffield plate maker.

Close-plating, the technique of applying silver foil by means of a hot soldering iron, was usually applied to iron or steel, but was also used on nickel-silver spoons for a short time after 1833 (see also Electroplate, page 20).

Top, left to right: Ladle, brass; French late 18th or early 19th century; unmarked; 14$\frac{1}{5}$ inches. Tablespoon, iron, traces of tinning; English c. 1820 or later; maker's mark: GAD or GAN and a sword. Tablespoon, Chinese or Japanese c. 1927; engraved with symbol for 'thunder' and 1927; although looks like plated copper, is actually low-grade silver; style typical of Far Eastern adaptations of fiddle. Tablespoon, Sheffield plate; Sheffield late 18th century; unmarked. Ladle, Sheffield plate; Sheffield late 18th century; unmarked.

Bottom, left to right: Two teaspoons, from set with sugar tongs; Sheffield (? or Birmingham) late 18th century; small and lightly constructed; unmarked. Teaspoon, brass; French 18th century; stamped PERFET; similar spoon is stamped PAR'FI AVRO. Egg spoon, gilt copper; Sheffield c. 1805; from Sheffield-plate egg stand; maker's mark of Goodman Gainsford and Fairbairn.

Later metals: pewter, Britannia, German silver

Pewter spoons found their best market among country dwellers of conservative bent who accepted well-established styles and felt no need to keep up with fashion. The spoon opposite was among the last to be made before the more durable Britannia-metal was adopted by Americans. Its fiddle-handle with pointed shoulders had been high style for about ten years and would continue so for another ten. The handle's feather-edging is a bit of a finery that would have been unusual on a silver spoon at the time, which would have had either a plain handle or a handle with only a shell, basket or sheaf for decoration.

Moulds for casting pewter objects were expensive, but fortunately for the spoonmaker they could be used for the new Britannia as well as for pewter. And, even more fortunately, Britannia could not only be stamped, but was soon found to make a satisfactory base for electroplating. It was rivalled in about 1840, however, by other metal alloys variously called German silver, albata, arguzoid, alfenide, argentan and argentine throughout the century. Made of one part nickel, one to two parts zinc, and three to four parts copper, German silver, developed in Germany before 1824, had shine and hardness, but it lacked the beauty of silver, and was therefore little accepted save as a base for electroplating.

After 1840, American pewterers and Britannia-makers were faced with the competition of inexpensive electroplated silver. In the 1870s, recognizing defeat in the market, they finally closed shop.

Teaspoon, pewter, c. 1820; cast downturned fiddle-end partially feather-edged, pointed shoulders and tapering pointed drop; maker's or owner's mark: P. DERR/1820 (Peter Derr, Berks County, Pennsylvania); $8\frac{7}{16}$ inches

English Britannia-metal

The 18th-century origins of Britannia-metal and its use in America, are described on pages 16 and 17. By the 1780s, it was being cast in England into inexpensive spoons, which, perhaps because of their cheapness (see Introduction), withstood the competition of electro-plated spoons until about 1900. J. B. Himsworth (see Bibliography) in 1884 'saw many gross of these spoons being cast in Bramall Lane, Sheffield, by a woman caster for Henry Holdsworth, a descendant of William Holdsworth'. Holdsworth is described in an 1825 directory as a 'Britannia Spoon Manufacturer, grocer and rag merchant', an indication of the trade's social level.

   Sheffield was the main production centre, and the firm of Philip Ashberry (1820s to 1860s) seems, on the evidence of spoons surviving, to have been the most prolific. Birmingham too was important, and the makers, John Yates and Thomas Yates, were responsible for most of the Britannia-metal spoons remaining in England. They also produced a great many for export to the United States. The spoons shown here, of continental shape with pointed stems, were perhaps also intended for export. The dark colouring on some of the spoons illustrated is the result of oxidation.

Ladle, Birmingham 1859 or later; hollow stem cast in three sections; marked THOS. YATES CROWN METAL *and registered design mark for 14 March 1859; $14\frac{1}{5}$ inches.*

Top, left to right: Tablespoon, English second half of 19th century; beaded Old English; no marks; $8\frac{1}{2}$ inches. Tablespoon, Sheffield perhaps c. 1825; pointed-end fiddle; marked ASHBERRY PATENT *beneath* G.R. *Tablespoon (back); Sheffield mid-19th century; fiddle; ridge on stem conceals strengthening steel wire; marked* ASHBERRY'S BEST METAL WARRANTED FOR USE *beneath* V.R. *and crown. Tablespoon, Birmingham 1851 or later; Old English diagonal ridges at end; back of stem plain; marked* THOMAS YATES SILVER METAL; *registered design mark for 13 Oct. 1851. Sauce ladle, Sheffield, mid-19th century; fiddle; marked* WOLSTENHOLM *and crown. Tablespoon (back), Sheffield c. 1830; plain Old English; marked* I. HARRISON NORFOLK WORKS SHEFFIELD, *and* PATENT *beneath* W R *and crown.*

Bottom, left to right: Teaspoon, Birmingham mid-19th century; Old English; marked John Yates *and* V R *beneath crown. Tablespoon, English early 19th century; pointed stem, turned up at end; marked* LONDON; *a second mark illegible. Tablespoon, Sheffield mid-19th century; ridged fiddle pattern; back of bowl cast with crude shell-like drop; maker, Ashberry, marked as wired fiddle, above.*

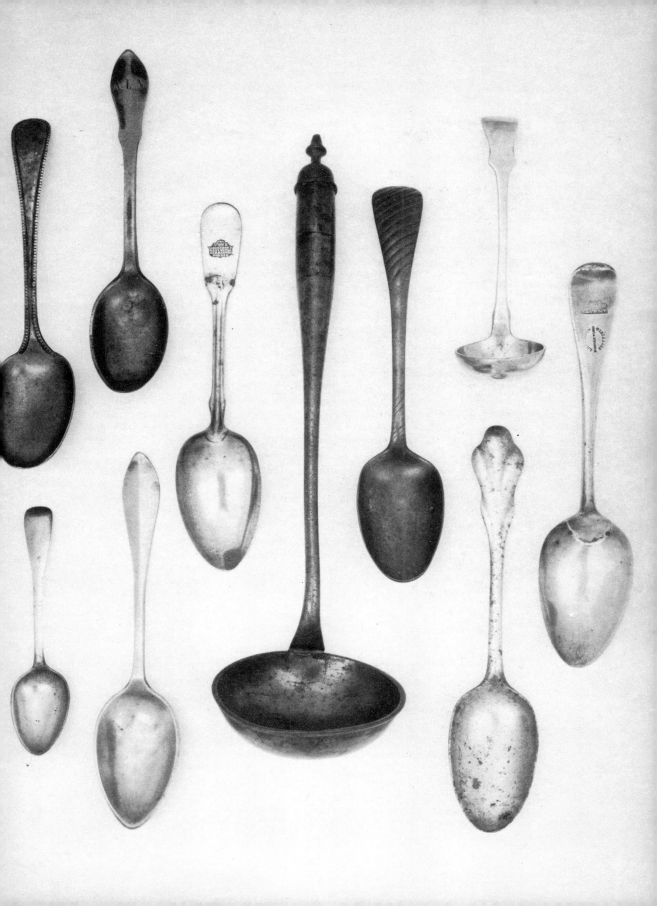

Electroplate

Several developments combined to bring the shine of silver by the middle of the 19th century to dining-rooms that had never before held sterling, Sheffield plate, or even 'Coin': Volta's discovery in 1794 of the principle of the electric battery; John Wright's and Brugnatelli's advances in electrolysis between 1800 and 1815; the advent in about 1836 of a dependable battery, and the application of all three in 1840 by the Elkingtons of Birmingham to the electrochemical depositing of silver on base metals.

The difference in cost between sterling and plated silver was eight or ten to one, not only because of the difference in the cost of the metals but also in the skill involved. Electroplate was even less expensive than plated silver, that money-saving sandwich of copper and silver first put together by Thomas Boulsover in about 1742 in Sheffield. Indistinguishable at first glance from thoroughgoing silver, both plated and electroplated silver pleased hearts and pocketbooks in England and America, and were considered acceptable until the price of sterling dropped with the opening of silver mines in the American West in the 1890s.

Americans who advertised 'silverplating', as did William Healy of Philadelphia as early as 1785, were neither bonding silver to copper nor, of course, practising electrolysis. They were using the process called close-plating—covering small metal objects with silver foil and borax and heating them red-hot to fuse the metals. (See page 14).

Plated silver was introduced into the United States by John O. Mead who brought it from Birmingham to Philadelphia in 1837, became a partner of Asa and William Rogers of Hartford, Connecticut in 1845, and there produced silver which they advertised in 1851 as 'plated on the best Quality cast steel . . . and on all kinds of metal to order'.

Left to right: Teaspoon, 1850-60; upturned fiddle-shell; maker's mark: W. ROGERS incuse a mark not previously published (Hartford, Connecticut); 5⅜ inches. Teaspoon, 1860-70, beaded pattern; maker's mark: J. STEVENSON incuse (John Stevenson, location unknown) 5¾ inches. Tablespoon, 1850-60; downturned fiddle-end with long rounded shoulders; maker's mark: F. CHAFFEE and eagle pseudo hall-mark in rectangles (possibly Hartford, Connecticut); 8½ inches. Mustard spoon, 1858; c 1840; upturned fiddle-tipped, flaring shoulders, fig-shaped bowl; maker's mark: P GARRETT & SON/A1 in rectangles (Philip Garrett Philadelphia, Pennsylvania); 5 5/16 inches.

Simple materials

Spoon-collecting is by no means limited to spoons of silver, pewter and Britannia-metal designed for the table. It can range far afield into spoons of copper, wood, horn, tin, brass and even iron, made for the kitchen. Manufacturers of iron and tin spoons advertised side by side with those who made spoons of silver, German silver, Britannia-metal and/or plated silver.

Americans had need of many implements of all grades of refinement throughout the 19th century. Dwellings ranged in comfort from Brussels-carpeted, gas-lit town houses to sod-houses on the plains lit by oil-lamps. It was a century of extremes—of the frontiersman, Kit Carson, and the visit of the aristocratic Marquis de Lafayette; of the siege of the Alamo and of luxurious Atlantic steamships; of the Pony Express and the transcontinental railway; of the Rough Riders and New York's wealthy society-leaders, 'The Four Hundred', and of spending new-found gold and silver.

A half-dozen Britannia, electroplate, or even silver spoons *might* have been among the treasures of the sod-house, but spoons of lesser materials, made in England, Europe or America, would surely have been there. Some of these, dating from the previous century, would have been behind the scenes in the great houses, as well.

When in 1830 Robert Scadin, a carpenter of Cooperstown, New York, charged William Nichols fifteen cents for 'making Patram for spoons', his customer may have been a silversmith, tinsmith, pewterer, brass founder or blacksmith. He may have been a maker of horn spoons, who would dry his softened animal horn over Scadin's pattern. The pattern may have moulded a spoon to be used for eating Indian pudding, stirring apple butter or sampling blueberry flummery; or for feeding an invalid, spooning gravy or skimming jam.

Left to right: Two wooden spoons, one incorporating butter print, Europe, 1700-1800; 9¼ inches. Copper measuring spoon, England or United States, 1700-1800; 12 inches. Wrought-iron, brass and copper spoon, United States, dated 1823; 13⅛ inches. Underneath: Horn spoon, probably England, 1775-1800; 10¾ inches.

Wood, bone and horn

Wood, bone and horn were probably the first materials to be deliberately shaped into spoons. Indeed, the word 'spoon' derives from the Old English, 'spon', meaning a chip of wood. By the 17th century, spoons of those materials were only for the poor, except for certain specialized types such as wooden (floating) punch ladles; after 1900 their general use largely ceased. Most 18th- and 19th-century spoons made of wood or horn can be divided into two main groups: metal shapes, often in such simplified utilitarian forms that they cannot be accurately dated or placed; and country-made spoons of traditional styles now recognized as 'folk art', and also difficult to date, because their designs are essentially conservative and unchanging.

The art of carving wooden spoons was particularly well developed by the peasants of northern Europe and Russia, who concentrated largely on the decoration of their stems, which were often extremely wide and elaborately pierced. Similar carving techniques in different areas tended to produce similar forms, but certain distinctive types did emerge. An abundance of thick leafy scrolls is, for instance, typical of spoons from Scandinavia. The unique Russian painted 'Khokhloma' ware named after its original centre of production in the Volga forests, and recently revived, is distinguished by its use of metallic colours and hard varnished finish. In many places, including Wales, England, Switzerland and Scandinavia, very elaborate and often entirely impracticable wooden spoons were carved by young men as love tokens.

Horn spoons—once used all over Europe but traditional in Scotland and still made there—are not carved, but formed by pressing between moulds a horn sheet which had previously been softened by heat.

Top: Horn spoon, Icelandic 19th century; stem engraved GBD.
Bottom, left to right: Spoon of stained birch wood, Scandinavian 18th or 19th century; carved openwork stem. Spoon of pressed horn (back), German 19th century; imitating metal forms; bowl back engraved with arms of Arnburg; inside, the inscription: 'Ex Cadem Stipite Prosper Fui'. Spoon of painted, gilded and varnished wood, modern Russian (probably Semyonov) 'Khokhloma' ware. Punch ladle of bone, probably Scottish 18th or 19th century; stem screws into bowl. Ladle of pressed horn, perhaps Scottish, second half 19th century; imitating metal forms; 11⅕ inches. Punch ladle, wood and silver, English mid-18th century, marks of London silversmith Edmund Medlicott. Spoon, pressed horn; European, 19th century; simple imitation of metal type.

Ceramics

Relative mass-production in the second half of the 18th century led to the widespread use of ceramic dinner and tea services, with easily replaceable pieces. In general, those who could afford porcelain could also afford silver flatware, so few spoons were made in costly porcelain, but many were produced for the less affluent in cheap earthenware. Porcelain sugar sifters with pierced bowls appeared on the Continent in the mid-18th century, and Bow and Worcester versions followed shortly afterwards; French tin-glazed and Chinese porcelain versions were also made. Sugar and tablespoons of inexpensive creamware were listed in the pattern books of Castleford (1796) and Leeds (1814); Wedgwood advertised egg and dessert spoons in 1774, and tablespoons as late as 1880.

Although ceramic spoons were ideal for foods such as eggs and mustard, which rapidly tarnished silver, they were—especially those made of brittle earthenware—easily broken and impossible to repair; very few survive. Ladles, because of their thick bowls and round stems, were stronger, and 19th-century Staffordshire blue-printed sauce and soup ladles are not uncommon—indeed they are still made.

In the late 18th century, caddy spoons of porcelain were made by the Derby, Caughley and Worcester factories, and specimens of black basalt in silver shapes, by Wedgwood. Worcester also copied the flat-bottomed, boat-shaped Chinese spoon, sometimes pierced to serve as a sugar sifter.

Top row, left to right: Ladle, Spode factory, 1825-33; blue-printed earthenware; the type continues in production; 5 inches. Soup ladle, earthenware, blue-printed Willow Pattern; Staffordshire, mid-19th century. Sauce ladle, Staffordshire late 18th century; cream ware with enamelling; some ladles of this type have yellow-enamelled bowls perhaps in imitation of gilding of salt-spoons. Sugar-spoon, Belgium (Tournai) second half 18th century; porcelain painted in blue; this style influenced spoons produced by English porcelain factories.

Middle row, left to right: Ladle for miniature sauce-boat; Staffordshire c. 1840; blue-printed earthenware. Ladle for miniature sauce-tureen; similar to mustard spoons, often supplied with pots. Sugar sifter, Staffordshire c. 1755; press-moulded salt-glazed stoneware; crispness of lead mould is well reproduced by fine stoneware and thin glaze, achieving elegance at expense of strength.

Bottom: Medicine spoon, porcelain; German early 19th century; English versions sometimes advertise the name of the chemist in the bowl; a graduated spoon patented by Maw Son & Thompson, 1873.

Techniques of manufacture

The steel dies used to put rat-tails, decorative drops and 'picture-backs' on the bowls of 17th- and 18th-century spoons were flat, engraved plates against which the flat spoon shape was struck.

The upper sequence opposite shows the technical advance which followed; the die-stamping of an entire spoon, probably used in France in the mid-18th century and generally adopted in England by 1800. The flat outline of the spoon—the blank—is at first forged by hammer, care being taken to increase the thickness in the parts to be decorated. The blank is then placed between engraved steel dies which are driven together with great force, producing stage 4.

The relief decoration is now in its final state, but the spoon has still to be trimmed, the bowl domed, the stem straightened and the whole finally polished.

Smaller dies were also used, which stamped designs on the upper stem or bowl only and could be struck together with a sledge hammer.

Blanks cut from sheet-silver soon replaced the considerably stronger forged type, and in the mid-19th century an ingenious machine was invented in which the blanks were given their decoration between engraved rollers. A common modern method, used for many metals, forms a rough blank by 'cross-rolling'. All the subsequent stamping operations are also performed by machine.

The lower sequence shows a modern revival—by a modern craftsman—of the method by which most English silver spoons were made until the advent of die-stamping. The flat shape of the spoon in outline is swiftly made from the silver ingot, using only a heavy spoon-making hammer. In stage 4 the spoon has reached its final hammered shape, and has been 'planished'—given a smooth surface with a polished hammer. It is now bowed in profile to facilitate the polishing and the final filing to shape. In the last steps the bowl is 'domed' in an appropriately shaped hollow made in a lump of lead, using a punch and hammer; the stem is straightened and the spoon given its final polish.

Top: Six stages in making a hand-forged and die-struck Albert pattern dessert spoon at C.J. Vander Ltd., London. The final spoon bears the London hall-marks for 1974. Initial ingot 4 inches long, 0.2 inches thick; final spoon $7\frac{1}{3}$ inches long. Bottom: Five stages of a hand-forged tablespoon made by R.K.N. Wilkins for Francis Cooper. The final spoon, $8\frac{1}{2}$ inches long, bears the London hall-marks for 1964. Initial ingot $3\frac{1}{5}$ inches long, $\frac{1}{5}$ inch thick.

Die-stamped decoration, intaglio and quality marks

The die press, which by the mid-19th century could turn out a spoon complete with three dimensions and an all-over pattern, did away with the necessity for forging and chasing. The silversmith needed only to heighten the stamped design with his chasing tools and to smooth the spoon's edges with his files.

New methods of die-cutting around 1800 had produced intaglio marks for makers' names. The die, instead of depressing a rectangular or oval background, leaving the letters to stand out from the surface, could cut the letters *into* the surface with no punch-shape showing around them. Thus it became possible completely to spell out the first name, middle initial and last name of the silversmith and/or retailer. Often the city, state, street and street number were included as well. Although this is uninteresting in appearance, it is a boon to the collector, enabling him to identify his spoon by maker and location.

Spoons of the 19th century often bore a word or numerals to suggest the quality of the metal of which they were made. The mark of a maker from the time of the earliest silversmithing in New England and in the 1670s has been considered his guarantee of quality in both metal and workmanship, and until 1792 no official standards had been imposed on the metal he used. In that year the United States mint established a standard for coin of 892.4 parts silver to 108 parts copper and other ingredients. Seven Baltimore silversmiths between 1800 and 1814 used STERLING in the manner of Irish silversmiths. Other silversmiths early in the century stamped such terms as Coin, Pure, Standard and Dollar on silver objects to advertise that the metal was at least of coin quality. In 1837 the standard was raised to 11 ounces Troy or 91.7 per cent silver.

An assay office had been opened by the Maryland legislature in 1814 at the instigation of customers who felt that silversmiths were not careful enough about using silver of coin standard. It functioned for sixteen years, the only period in the United States during which quality marks, city marks and date letters were rationalized and strictly enforced. Before and after the existence of the assay office, Baltimore silversmiths used '11 oz' or '10.15 oz' to indicate a metal content of 11 or 10.15 ounces of silver per 12 ounces of Troy weight.

Salt spoon, c. 1850; beaded pattern double face; hemispherical bowl fluted around plain reserve; maker's mark: JONES BALL & Co/incised (Boston, Massachusetts); $3\frac{3}{16}$ inches.

Bowl backs

The backs of spoon bowls, like spoon handles, could be enriched with raised designs by setting the spoon face downwards in sand or on a slab of lead, placing against it a die cast with the design, and striking the die with a hammer. The sand or soft lead gave with the blow and allowed the spoon to keep its shape, while the pattern appeared on the bowl back.

Eighteenth-century decoration was more plentiful and varied than that of the 19th century. Ridged and beaded rat-tails and airy scrolls appeared between 1700 and 1730, and shells, birds, or foliate scrolls between 1730 and 1800. They all surpassed in number and in beauty the occasional urn, shell, or eagle of 1800-30. In addition to decoration, spoon backs bore rat-tails between 1700 and 1750, or drops, or both, from 1750 to 1770.

The drop continued into the 19th century, often in raised versions. The standard raised drop was short and rounded, but there were many variations: long, double, broad, oval, tapering, pointed and pointed-arched. The surface of all these shapes could be modelled. The long drop, for instance, was frequently scored near the tip with a line or a V. Although the standard drop persisted until 1810, degenerate forms appeared simultaneously.

Spoons decorated with symbolic or political devices are 'fancy backs'; often different makers used the same device, which suggests that they may have traded dies, or used dies by the same engraver.

Left to right: Teaspoon, 1810-20; downturned narrow fiddle-end; incised pointed-arch drop and eagle with shield on bowl back; maker's mark: T. C. & H. in rectangle (unknown); 5¾ inches. Dessert spoon, 1830-40; downturned fiddle tipped with short vestigial midrib, wide flaring shoulders on bowl back; maker's mark: P. P. HAYES/PO' KEEPSIE incuse with bust and étoile in circles (Peter P. Hayes, Poughkeepsie, New York); 6¹³⁄₁₆ inches. Teaspoon, c. 1825; broad downturned fiddle-end pointed shoulders, pointed bowl with pointed drop and draped urn; maker's mark: WMB/READING in rectangle (William Mannerback, Reading, Pennsylvania); 5³⁄₁₆ inches. Teaspoon, 1824-27; downturned fiddle-end, short pointed shoulders, plain drop; maker's mark: NH in oval; Baltimore shield in clipped rectangle and C in square for 1824-27 (Nicholas Hutchins, Baltimore, Maryland); 5⁷⁄₁₆ inches. Tablespoon, 1805-10; coffin fiddle-end, short square shoulders, oval modelled drop; maker's mark: A & G WELLES in rectangle (Alfred and George Welles, Boston, Massachusetts); 7¾ inches.

Maker's mark

The backs of spoons are interesting even more for their makers' marks than for their decorations or drops. Marks differ greatly and the collector examines each carefully. What, in the first place, is the background, that is the outline or shape of the punch? In the period from 1670 to 1730 it was a shield, trefoil or quatrefoil. Between 1730 and 1830 it became a rectangle, oval, cartouche, ribbon or annulet. Most craftsmen used the rectangle with a plain outline, but there were variations, with the outline stepped, serrated, engrailed (notched or indented) or barbed; its corners could be clipped, or it could conform to the shape of what it enclosed.

The letters which a silversmith or engraver chose reveal a great deal about his character, skill and taste. They may be in a straight line, regular and with finely executed serifs and pleasing spaces; or they may be crude and irregular. They may be Roman capitals of one size or of two sizes; they may be script or italic. The punctuation may be full stops (periods) or pellets, which are full stops raised above the base line. Sometimes such small devices as stars, *étoiles,* plus-signs and colons were substituted for full stops and pellets.

These marks were gradually supplanted after 1800 by incuse marks of machine-like regularity, which lacked a background and the character that comes with hand-work.

Left to right: Teaspoon 1795-1805; coffin-end with double roulette, or wrigglework, V drop; maker's mark: W. SIME in script in oval (Portsmouth, New Hampshire); $5\frac{3}{16}$ inches. Tablespoon, 1790-1800; rounded downturned with vestigial midrib on handle back, bright-cut handle decoration, incised V drop; maker's mark: HUTTON in rectangle (Isaac Hutton, Albany, New York); 9 inches. Tablespoon, 1805-10; downturned shoulderless coffin fiddle-end, with incised pointed-arch drop; maker's mark: IPT in script in oval (John Proctor Trott, New London, Connecticut); $9\frac{1}{4}$ inches. Tablespoon, 1810-20; downturned coffin fiddle-end with bright-cut decoration and incised crescent drop; maker's mark: L RYERSON in script in stepped rectangle (York, Pennsylvania); $9\frac{7}{16}$ inches.

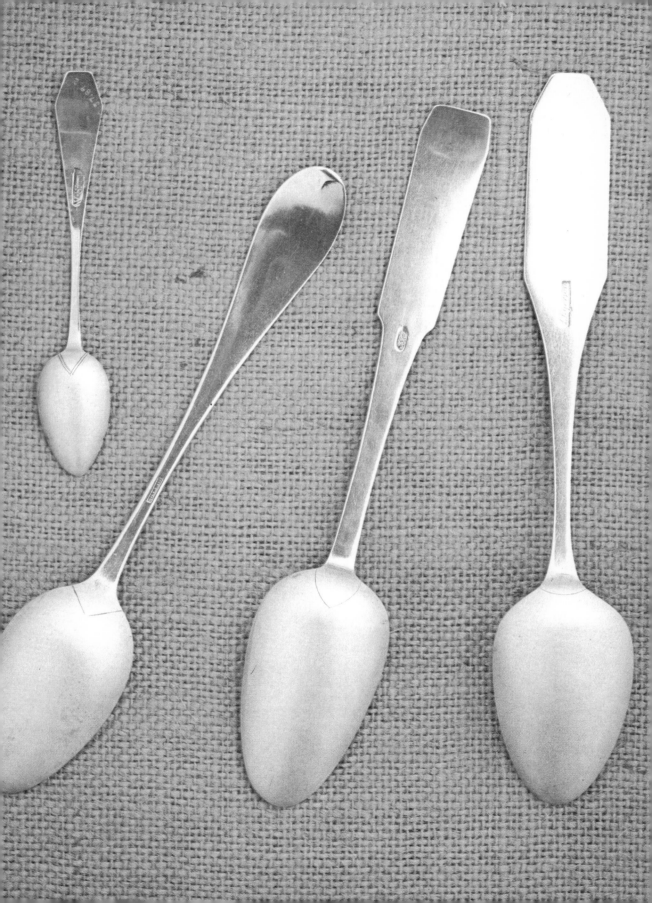

Machines and 19th-century spoonmakers' practices

The rapid advance of industrialization in the 19th century enabled spoonmakers, as it did other artisans, to accomplish intricate tasks with ease and speed. The age, in general, was happy with its machines and with the uniform high-standard articles they made. 'Ingenuity of the age,' wrote an anonymous contented consumer in the *New England Business Directory* for 1856, 'produces articles which by their simplicity and beauty of construction, perfection and accuracy of execution, are not only the pride and glory of the artisan, but are of indispensable utility.'

Among the processes and inventions which made possible the production in quantity of the beautiful, the utilitarian and the economical were Maudslay's metal lathe, the first to have a holding-rack for the turner's tool; steam power attached to die-stamping machines; coke and compressed-air blasts for smelting iron, and the development of harder steel for pattern dies.

Designers of spoons, no longer inhibited by the need for expensive hand-labour, drew inspiration from many sources, among them the botanical world and the rococo of the preceding century. Silver-spoon manufacturers drew freely also from the designs of their neighbours and competitors, virtually copying each other's popular patterns or pattern names throughout the century. This relaxed practice was reflected in the lack of care given to preserving the original maker's identity. Spoons made by one firm were bought unmarked by another and marked with the buyer's (dealer's) name. They were then put on the market. Maker's marks were stamped over with buyer's or dealer's marks, or placed side by side with them. Because both buyer and maker were manufacturers of silver spoons, the baffled collector is left to deduce which was which.

Left to right: Teaspoon, 1860-70; wreath pattern; maker's mark: M. S. SMITH & Co incuse (Martin S. Smith, Detroit, Michigan); $5\frac{5}{8}$ inches. Teaspoon, 1860-70; ivy pattern, double face; maker's mark: SQUIRE & LANDER/STERLING (Bela S. Squire, Jr. & Horatio N. Squire & Tobias D. Lander, New York, New York); $8\frac{1}{4}$ inches. Teaspoon, 1845-52; knotted-thread design, double-swell fiddle-end with raised edge knotted at tip of handle and top of stem, double face; maker's mark: TENNEY (William I. Tenney, New York, New York); $6\frac{1}{2}$ inches. Teaspoon, 1858; Chippendale pattern; maker's mark: G & S in oval, 1858 in lozenge (William Gale and Son, William Jr., New York, New York); dealer's mark: G. LOOMIS/ERIE (Guy Loomis, Pennsylvania); $8\frac{5}{16}$ inches.

English design 1660-1800

The first modern form, the trifid, with a notched stem, originated in France, reached England by 1662 and remained in use until about 1700. It was followed by a short-lived, but subsequently much copied, wavy-ended stem, which by 1710 had given way to the Hanoverian stem, with a rounded and *turned up* end. Trifid bowls were the first with a ridge or 'rat-tail', a fashion replaced in about 1730 by single or double-drops or 'heels'. The double-drop was the most popular until after 1800; from the 1740s to the 1790s bowls, particularly those of teaspoons, also bore stamped ornament.

The Hanoverian stem survived into the 1780s, but was gradually replaced from the 1760s by the Old English stem, with a rounded and *turned down* end, and sometimes decorated with beading, threading, or feather edging, or with bright-cut engraving. The Onslow stem, with a scroll-end, was typical of the 1760s, but much copied later. The plain fiddle pattern with bevelled edge was a French design. Taken up in England in about 1800, it, together with its more elaborate variations (page 46), became the basic pattern for plain metal spoons for the next century. Old English, however, never fell out of use, but adopted the bevelled edge, and from about 1800 to about 1830 shared with the plain fiddle the widely spreading stem and upturned pointed bowl of French Empire designs.

Flatware gradually increased in size up to 1800, as the spoons illustrated (tablespoons unless otherwise specified) demonstrate.

Top, left to right: Trifid spoon, London 1670; back, showing rat-tail; maker's mark: IK with a rose and two pellets. Dessert spoon, London 1703; wavy-ended or 'dog-nose' stem; maker, John Ladyman. Hanoverian, London 1722; back, showing rat-tail; maker, Edward Jennings. Hanoverian, London 1744; maker's mark: J.W. in script. Hanoverian, London 1761; back, showing double-drop; maker's mark: W.L. Hanoverian, London 1750; back, showing shell; maker's mark: R.H. Old English, London 1777; back, showing shell and scroll; maker, Hester Bateman. (Below) Mote spoon, London 1777.

Bottom, left to right: Old English stem, (?) London c. 1770; feathered edge and shell; marks illegible. Old English, London 1776; bright-cut engraved; maker, Hester Bateman. Old English, London 1793; makers, Peter and Ann Bateman; made as plain spoon; converted into 'berry spoon' in 19th century by embossing decoration in bowl and engraving stem. Old English, London 1816; bevelled edge; makers, S. and J.W. Blake; $7\frac{9}{10}$ inches. Old English (back), London 1805; bevelled edge, single drop; maker's mark: S.H. Dessert spoon (back), Birmingham, 1846; mark: EPNS; plain fiddle pattern; maker, Elkington, Mason and Co. Plain fiddle pattern, Jersey, inscribed 1828.

A forerunner

In the 1770s when the upturned midrib Hanoverian spoon was going out of fashion in the colonies and the downturned rounded Old English spoon was gaining favour, a short-lived transitional style, which lasted only for about a decade, was made by a small number of American and English silversmiths. But it foreshadowed the 19th century. Its handle was downturned, its bowl was the old ellipse, and, at the joining of the bowl and handle, two small shoulders or fins projected—an adaptation of a spoon which had furnished French dining tables since the late 17th century. Why these shoulders should have been dropped after so brief a period, only to be revised again in 1810, has never been satisfactorily explained.

Among their early American makers was the famous Revolutionary patriot, Paul Revere. The son of Appollos Rivoire, a Huguenot refugee, he was born in 1735 and worked in Boston between 1755 and 1818 as one of the third generation of colonial silversmiths. The first, in the late 17th century, were John Hull, Robert Sanderson, Jeremiah Dummer and John Coney, whose handsome silver vessels and spoons now grace New England museums.

Revere's shouldered spoons were either feather-edged, with beaded foliate scrolls on the bowl backs, or had plain or bright-cut handles, with ridged, shell-like bowls. The Sargent family of Boston ordered a dozen teaspoons and a dozen tablespoons of the former style engraved with their leaping-dolphin family crest. Revere in 1787 charged Nathaniel Austin, himself a silversmith, £2 for making a dozen of the latter style.

Teaspoon by Paul Revere 1772; rounded downturned feather-edge, straight shoulders, crest of Sargent family in cartouche on handle front, beaded foliate scroll and drop on bowl back; maker's mark: P R in script in rectangle (Paul Revere, Boston, Massachusetts); $\cdot5\frac{3}{4}$ inches.

Early French patterns

The chief French contribution to flatware is the fiddle pattern, which first appeared in a primitive form in the late 17th century. By the middle of the 18th, the modern plain fiddle was established, as were the types decorated with shells and threaded edges. The fiddle-thread or *modèle à filets* has remained immensely popular. A long tapering shoulder at the bowl characterizes the French fiddle form. At the same time, a number of less long-lived variations emerged, which had considerable influence elsewhere. In these the wider end of the stem was waisted, and given more or less elaborate relief ornament. This style, the French themselves called, from its shape, the *modèle à violon*—literally, fiddle—and they refer only to the waisted type by this name. Simpler French fiddle spoons are often large and very heavy. In the late 18th and first half of the 19th centuries, they had heavy, pointed, sharply upturned bowls.

A straight rounded-end stem was developed in the 18th century, which, when stamped with restrained neo-classical ornament, became typical of the First Empire (the two silver-gilt spoons illustrated). Later 19th-century French flatware continued on the whole to be of restrained design, and after 1850 consisted largely of revivals of First Empire, neo-classical (Louis XVI) and lightly treated rococo (Louis XV) patterns, as in the spoon opposite.

The baguette pattern, which has an entirely plain back, was first produced by the firm Christofle (see Introduction) in 1861, and became popular everywhere except Britain and Scandinavia.

Top, left to right: Tablespoon (?) c. 1900; EPNS; baguette pattern; stamped metal blanc *and 84 gr. below unidentified symbol. Dessert spoon, Paris 1819-38; silver-gilt; maker, François Dominique Naudin. Dessert spoon, Paris 1798-1809; silver-gilt; maker, Pierre Benôit Lorrillon; 7½ inches. Dessert spoon (?) Paris second half 19th century; en suite* with fork; silver with porcelain handle; maker's mark: G.D. in lozenge with spoon, caduceus and rosette. Dessert spoon, probably Paris c. 1890; from christening set; maker's mark: PQ, unidentified. Dessert spoon, c. 1900 or later; EPNS; Louis XV pattern; stamped ERCUIS and OE above centaur, 60 below.*

Bottom, left to right: Service, modèle à filets*: tea, dessert, table, serving spoon; dessert spoon, 1819-38, maker, probably Bazile Chenailler, Paris. 7 inches. All others, Paris 1809-19; maker's mark: T B L, unidentified. Soup ladle, c. 1900 or later; EPNS; maker, Orfèvrerie Christofle, Paris; stamped ALFENIDE, CC in a lozenge, 74 and CHRISTOFLE.*

Holdovers from the 18th century

A collector finds it difficult to establish a national difference between English and American silver spoons simply by looking at them. The reason is not hard to find: American silver spoons, like most American domestic silver, were based on those of the wealthy middle-class Englishman. By the 1800s, however, the only holdovers from the previous century were a solely American coffin-end and the pointed, rounded or oval (plain or bright-cut) Old English style common to England and her colonies.

In spite of the need Americans felt for independence from Great Britain, they clung to London styles and welcomed them in spoons as in clothes and furniture, adopting each innovation as it reached them. Spoons developed in a progression from the flat, straight-handled examples with elliptical bowls and trifid or wavy ends of the Stuart/Hanoverian period (1670-1730), through the upturned midrib Hanoverian variety with round-in-section stems and rat-tail bowls of 1730-70, to the downturned rounded- or oval-end Old English of the last quarter of the 18th century. Americans welcomed especially variations of feather-edging and of bright-cutting on the Old English style, and produced a coffin-end variation of their own between 1785 and 1810 by clipping the round or oval ends of plain Old English spoons to save time and effort.

Four tablespoons made in New York and Connecticut engraved with their owners' initials in intertwined script, a fashion dating from the 1780s. Left to right: Coffin-end, 1805-13; maker's mark: HART & WILCOX in rectangle (Judah Hart and Alvin Wilcox, Norwich, Connecticut); $9\frac{9}{16}$ inches. Pointed downturned handle, raised, pointed-arch drop on bowl back, 1805-13; maker's mark: T. KEELER in rectangle (Thaddeus Keeler, New York, New York and Norwalk, Connecticut); $9\frac{1}{2}$ inches. Rounded downturned, 1802-10; maker's mark: M M & Co in serrated rectangle (Marcus Merriman, New Haven, Connecticut); $8\frac{7}{8}$ inches. Bright-cut handle, 1807-10; maker's mark: I. KETCHAM in rectangle (James Ketcham, New York, New York); 9 inches.

English patterns 1800-30

'Massiveness' was described in 1806 by the architect H. C. Tatham, author of an influential book on silver design, as 'the chief characteristic of good plate'. In order to achieve this quality, English spoonmakers turned, in about 1800, to the 18th-century French fiddle-pattern shapes, with their characteristic threaded edges and shells, which had already occasionally been copied in England and were widely imitated on the Continent. The manufacturing technique of striking in dies began to be used on a large scale in England at the same time. All the spoons shown here, except for the travelling spoon, are double-struck, with the design on both sides of the stem.

The simple fiddle-thread and fiddle-thread-and-shell patterns immediately became very popular and have remained so ever since. The curving hourglass pattern was a direct copy of a French original, and although it was short-lived in England, it was the basis of the King's pattern, an English design which appeared about 1815, together with the related Queen's or rosette pattern. The King's pattern was immensely popular in England throughout the 19th century and was widely imitated abroad.

The royal goldsmiths, Rundell, Bridge and Rundell, for whom the famous silversmith Paul Storr worked until 1819, originated the notable and ornate Coburg, Bacchanalian and stag hunt patterns, examples of which had entered the royal plate by 1812, 1812 and 1813 respectively. The last two were designed by the painter and draughtsman, Thomas Stothard, RA (1755-1834), and the stag hunt was probably modelled by the sculptor, Sir Francis Chantrey, RA (1781-1841).

Top, left to right: Dessert spoon (back), London 1866; makers, Henry Lias I and II. Dessert spoon (back), London 1868; military fiddle-thread; makers, G.W. Adams. Dessert spoon (back), London c. 1870; fiddle-thread and shell; maker's mark only, of Francis Higgins. Teaspoon, London 1873; military shell; maker's mark illegible. Tablespoon, London 1837; King's pattern; maker's mark illegible; $8\frac{7}{16}$ inches. Dessert spoon (back), London 1897; hourglass pattern; maker's mark: TS/WS/HH. Dessert spoon (back), London c. 1850; Queen's or rosette pattern; maker's mark only, of G.W. Adams. Dessert spoon (back), London 1840; shell and husk pattern.

Below, top to bottom: Travelling spoon (back), London 1825; silver-gilt; maker, George Reid; copy of spoon set, c. 1680. Dessert spoon (back), London c. 1850; pierced vine pattern; maker's mark only, of G.W. Adams. Dessert spoon, London 1816; Bacchanalian pattern; maker, Paul Storr. Gravy spoon, London 1816; stag hunt pattern; maker, Paul Storr.

Early fiddle-handles

The broad-handled spoon with narrow-shouldered stem—the 'fiddle' as it came to be called—which derived from the French and which showed itself briefly in America and in England in the 1770s, grew popular in both countries in the early 1800s. In the 'hourglass' pattern the British quickly adapted the threaded bordering and the double-swell outline of the several French *modèles à violon*, but the Americans resisted the trend until about 1820. All that they made when the style re-emerged was a straight-sided undecorated interpretation with a narrow rectangular handle and a flat stem which lacked shoulders entirely or bore only small pointed or straight ones. Light in weight, the American spoon was engraved across the handle-front with the initials of owners, either in the block lettering used in the 18th century, or in script capitals.

The American silversmith at the beginning of the 19th century was taking partners more often than he had in the 18th, and was also forming companies. He joined forces with watchmakers and clock-makers to import gold, silver, and jewellery from abroad or from other United States cities and towns, and to engage in retailing more intensively than before. Selling his own spoons directly, he had, as early as the 1780s, been shrewd about marketing methods, often enhancing the appeal of his wares to admirers of British-made objects by using pseudo-hallmarks beside his maker's mark. He simulated the letter and bust of British date; the lion which guaranteed sterling quality; the leopard's face which suggested that the object was assayed in London, and imitated other British city marks as well. Sometimes he substituted eagles, stars, *étoiles*, wheat-sheaves, or flowers, and, less frequently, buffalo, Indians or elephants.

Left to right: Teaspoon, 1816-18; shoulderless downturned fiddle-end; maker's mark: HALL & BLISS in serrated rectangle, and sheaf of wheat in rectangle (Albany, New York); $5\frac{1}{4}$ inches. Teaspoon, c. 1815; narrow downturned fiddle-end, rounded shoulders; maker's mark: B in clipped rectangle flanked by eagle and Indian in ovals (attributed to Theophilus Bradbury II, Newburyport, Massachusetts); $5\frac{9}{16}$ inches. Ice-cream spoon, 1830-40; downturned fiddle-end, slight midrib, long pointed shoulders, maker's mark: HILDEBURN/&/WATSON curved in oval, flanked by eagles in ovals (Samuel Hildeburn & James Watson, Philadelphia, Pennsylvania); $6\frac{1}{4}$ inches.

Scottish and Irish design

Irish and Scottish spoons of the 18th and 19th centuries followed English patterns, but with some striking variations. The English fiddle was the most popular 19th-century pattern both in Ireland, where the bowl was sometimes given a rat-tail, and in Scotland, where it adopted the long Scottish 'oar-ended' stem. The true Scottish oar-end spoon lacked the shoulders present on the fiddle and was current in the first half of the century. The so-called Scottish fiddle was waisted, echoing German and Danish styles, and was used for teaspoons during the second half of the 18th century.

The pointed-end spoon, with a markedly long stem turned down at the end, dominated Scottish flatware from about 1780 to 1820 and Irish, from about 1780 to 1800. In Ireland it was often engraved with bright-cut ornament, the Prince of Wales feather design, for instance, being peculiar to Cork. Later Scottish and Irish spoons tended to be more lightly constructed than English, except for serving or hash spoons, which could be as long as sixteen inches.

Top, Irish, left to right: Tablespoon, Dublin 1804; maker, John Kerns. Dessert spoon, Cork c. 1790; pointed end. Old English, bright-cut engraved with Prince of Wales' feathers; maker, Thomas Burke. (?) Mustard and pepper ladles (two), Cork c. 1795; pointed Old English, bright-cut engraved; crude holes in first possibly punched later; maker, William Teulon. Salt shovel, Dublin 1843; fiddle; maker, C. Cummins. Salt shovel, Dublin 1807 or 1808; fiddle-shell; maker, Samuel Neville. Two teaspoons (back and front), Dublin c. 1736; Hanoverian, rat-tails; Harp and Hibernia marks only. Egg spoon, Dublin 1818; Old English, no drop; maker, James Scott. Tablespoon, Dublin 1765; Onslow pattern, fluted bowl; maker, David Peter.

Bottom, Scottish, left to right: Tablespoon, Perth c. 1810; oar-ended fiddle, single drop; maker, William Ritchie; $9\frac{1}{10}$ inches. (?) Sugar spoon, Elgin c. 1810; elongated fiddle, no drop; maker, William Stephen Fergusson. Teaspoon, Dundee c. 1810; long oar-ended, single drop; maker, William Constable. Sauce ladle, Perth c. 1820; fiddle, no drop; maker, Robert Keay Sr. Hash spoon, Forres c. 1820; fiddle, single drop; makers, John and Patrick Riach; $11\frac{7}{10}$ inches. Toddy ladle, Dumfries c. 1830; twisted whalebone stem; maker, David Gray. Two teaspoons (front and back), Edinburgh c. 1760; Scottish fiddle, faceted double-drop; maker's mark only: John Welsh. Sauce ladle, Edinburgh 1855; flat-bottomed bowl, narrow round stem; maker's mark illegible. Teaspoon, Aberdeen c. 1790; Old English, engraved, single drop; maker, John Leslie. Tablespoon, Dundee c. 1740; Hanoverian; maker, John Steven.

Northern Europe: Russia and Norway

During the second half of the 19th century there was a general revival in Europe of old techniques for enamelling on metal. These included two methods using translucent enamel: *plique-à-jour*, in which the enamel is enclosed by metal frames, to produce a stained-glass effect; and *basse-taille*, in which the enamel is laid over engraved metal, permitting the engraving to show through. Two systems using opaque enamel also re-emerged: *cloisonné*, where the enamel is contained by metal strips in units or *cloisons*; and *champlevé*, where the enamel is contained in cavities in the background metal.

Cloisonné, the leading metalwork art-form in Russia in the 16th and 17th centuries, re-appeared there in the mid-19th, as an expression of nationalistic historicism (page 66). It was practised extensively by a school of skilful enamellers based in Moscow, most of whose surviving products date from the late 19th and early 20th centuries. Their *cloisons* are usually formed of wire filigree and strongly, almost gaudily, coloured in patterns derived from old Russian enamels, architecture and manuscripts. These enamels were frequently used on spoon-forms (centre opposite) adapted from 17th-century originals. The type was widely imitated in western Europe, and such 'fancy' spoons appeared in the design books of the Birmingham firm of Elkington, as early as 1857. Modern Russian enamels are considerably simpler.

Plique-à-jour was initially revived in France and was also practised in Russia, but was probably produced in the greatest quantity in Norway from the 1870s. The Norwegians usually used filigree surrounds of great delicacy, even in the numerous souvenir spoons they made for tourists in the years around 1900. *Cloisonné* very similar to that produced in Russia was also made in Norway, but with Viking-derived historicist motifs. A nationalistic Viking-type interlace ornament was also much used on silver spoons throughout Scandinavia in the late 19th and early 20th centuries (page 56).

Left to right: Coffee spoon, Russian (Leningrad) after 1958; silver-gilt, blue and green basse-taille *enamel; plain back; unidentified maker's mark* 2ЛЮ *. Coffee spoon, Norwegian c. 1900; silver with traces of gilding, stem of twisted wire decorated with translucent* plique à jour *enamel set in filigree; marked* MH *and 900, probably for Marius Hammer of Bergen; also stamped with a Swedish control mark. Spoon (back), Russian (Moscow) c. 1905; silver-gilt,* cloisonné filigree *enamel; maker, Nicolai Nicholaivich Zverev; 8 inches. Coffee spoon, Russian (Moscow) 1893; silver with traces of gilding; maker's mark illegible. Teaspoon, Russian (probably Leningrad) c. 1960; silver, blue and white* champlevé *enamel; plain back, marked* ЛЮ8M *and* МЕΛ6X *.*

Dutch design

Dutch spoons of the 18th and 19th centuries were, on the whole, modified versions of French or English spoon designs, with some exceptions: curved-stem cream ladles with round bowls; 19th-century spoons with curved stems of thin sheet silver (tea and caddy spoons illustrated); and traditional styles, unchanged since the late 17th century, often made as christening gifts. These last, manufactured until after 1900, had twisted or interlaced stems, finials formed as apostles, virtues, etc., and wide, square-shouldered bowls.

From the mid-19th century, they attracted the attention of spoonmakers in other countries, who believed them to be old and copied or adapted them. Concurrently, the Dutch themselves began to stamp such spoons with false marks that suggested the 17th century, and even to export them. They can be recognized by their crude finish and by the marks, which are large and lightly struck. The genuine (very small) maker's and standard marks are often present as well.

Top, left to right: Fruit spoon, Indian (Madras) c. 1860; from set; Dutch-type stem, figure of Hindu god, Narasinha; gilt bowl engraved with representation of Vishnu; engraved maker's mark: ORR (Peter N. Orr). Spoon, Dutch late 19th century; poorly-cast stem, finial figure of Hope; 17th-century form; $6\frac{9}{10}$ inches. Spoon, Dutch probably late 19th century; diamond-section stem; figure of Vanity; false mark only (?H below symbol). Birth spoon, Dutch (perhaps Groningen) second half 19th century; figure of Charity with three children; 17th-century form; false marks: HS monogram, L, and 5 over T.

Middle, left to right: Sugar sifter, Dutch 1814; gilt bowl, bone and ebony handle; maker, probably L. Koster. Apostle teaspoon, Dutch early 20th century; maker, probably Seton of Schoonhoven. Long teaspoon, Dutch 19th century; Cupid finial; unmarked. Long teaspoon, Dutch 19th century; cow finial; maker's mark: G and unidentified symbol. Teaspoon, Dutch late 19th century; sailing-boat finial, relief country scene on bowl; maker, Roelfsma of Winsum (two false marks). Caddy spoon, Dutch 1862; maker's mark illegible. Teaspoon, Amsterdam 1846; maker, H.A. Schuss.

Bottom, left to right: Cream ladle, Dutch early 19th century; embossed bowl; on stem, openwork relief of two putti; marked W and 20. Ladle, Dutch 17th or 18th century; hoof-shaped finial; unmarked. Cream ladle, Dutch 18th century; maker, probably Serp Swerms of Harlingen.

Northern Europe: Germany and Scandinavia

Northern European flatware of the 18th and 19th centuries was much influenced by French models. Typical is a design of the middle of the 18th century which, adopted in Sweden as *Gammalfransk* (old French), became its most popular 19th-century style (centre). Denmark, by the 1760s, had borrowed the French waisted fiddle and, in the following century, turned this style into its own classic. The plain fiddle also had a strong hold in the Germanic countries, but with variations: pronounced shoulders at the bowl, a wide-ended stem and a pointed bowl. German and Scandinavian fiddle and pointed-end spoons are frequently extremely light, with their bowls either plain or simply engraved with drops.

Spoons with pointed stems occurred simultaneously in Scandinavia, Holland and Germany at the end of the 18th century, and persisted through the 19th. The form appears to be a modification of Old English and is often bright-cut in the English manner.

King's pattern, Old English and Hanoverian were also widely copied. A continental version of the last, with a stem that has a wide end and a narrow, rounded section curving strongly down to the bowl, had appeared by the mid-18th century. During the 19th, it became a standard Dutch and German design, and was also adapted for the baguette pattern.

Centre: Serving spoon, Swedish (Falun) 1855; double-struck; engraved drop; maker, Carl Herdin; 10⁶⁄₁₀ inches.

Top, left to right: Tablespoon, Danish (Copenhagen) 1911; maker, Otto Friis. Tablespoon, Swedish (Stockholm) 1915; double-struck; maker's mark: A.G.D. Tablespoon, Swedish (Stockholm) 1874; King's pattern; double-struck; maker, S. Petterson. Tablespoon, Zürich early 19th century; plain back; engraved drop; maker's mark: IE. Teaspoon, German (probably Göttingen) c. 1914; Jugendstil; maker, A. Knauer; 5⁷⁄₁₀ inches. Tablespoon, German c. 1900; double-struck stem, Empire-revival; 800 standard mark.

Bottom, left to right: Dessert spoon, Swedish (Stockholm) 1911; Empire-revival; maker's mark: CS; 8⁷⁄₁₀ inches. Child's spoon, Swedish (Uppsala) 1946; maker's mark: M.G.AB; 5⁶⁄₁₀ inches. Teaspoon, Norwegian (Bergen) 1827; Old English; engraved front; maker, P.S. Kahrs. Tablespoon, Norwegian (Bergen) 1841; plain back; stem possibly shortened; maker, H.J. Blytt. Dessert spoon, German c. 1905; double-struck stem; Empire revival touch of Jugendstil; 800 standard mark; (?) maker's mark: a torch. Teaspoon, German mid-19th century; fiddle, plain back, pronounced shoulders; 13 Lot standard mark; maker's mark: R. GRUNDLER. Tablespoon, Prussian (Königsberg: now Kaliningrad, Lithuania) 1856.

American Fiddle-handles, 1810-60

Despite the increase in industrial power and the advent of better tools during the first half of the 19th century, both of which made easier the reproduction of elaborate styles, the simple fiddle patterns with variations on the handle and the stem had a long life. Makers from Rhode Island to Illinois rang changes on the handle in numerous ways: turning the end up instead of down, stamping it with a dog-nose, broadening it, rounding it, making it oval, giving it a double-swell outline or edging it with the raised line of the French thread-pattern. Modifications on the stem included making the cross-section round or rectangular and adding small fins or shoulders.

Shoulders themselves varied greatly, assuming outlines that can be described only inadequately as round, flaring, short, long, straight, squared or bevelled. In the United States in general, very small, pointed shoulders were made between 1800 and 1810. A sugar-loaf shape was made in Utica, New York, as well as in New York City and across the Long Island Sound in Connecticut, from 1820 to 1840. Long, rather flamboyant shoulders were made between 1840 and 1860. Otherwise, there seem to have been neither regional preferences nor chronological progression in shoulder styles.

The fiddle-end and its variations appeared in tablespoons, tea, soup, dessert, mustard, salt and gravy spoons, all of which had been introduced in the 18th century. Full services of flatware were first introduced in the 1780s, at about the same time as the first dinnerware services, and included all those forms. Although the number seems large, it was nothing compared with the deluge of new shapes that was to come after 1860.

Left to right: Sugar shell, 1841-42; upturned double-swell fiddle, tipped rounded shoulders; maker's mark: D. B. BLAKE & CO./PROVIDENCE R.I. in concave-cornered double-outline rectangles; 6 inches. Mustard ladle, 1835-50; upturned fiddle-thread, double face, gilded bowl, maker's mark: JACCARD & CO./ST. LOUIS in rectangles; $5\frac{5}{8}$ inches. Teaspoon, 1815; broad downturned fiddle-end with flaring shoulders; maker's mark: S. W. LEE in rectangle (Samuel W. Lee, Providence, Rhode Island to 1819 and Rochester, New York 1819-c. 1850); $5\frac{5}{16}$ inches. Mustard shell, 1846-48; oval fiddle-end with flaring shoulders tipped with dog-nose; maker's mark: L. NOWLIN/CHICAGO, ILL. incised; $5\frac{1}{4}$ inches. Teaspoon, 1845-55; upturned, tipped fiddle-end with rounded shoulders; maker's mark: THOMAS PERRY/PURE coin in double outline rectangle with concave corners; Westerly, Rhode Island in rectangles; $6\frac{3}{16}$ inches.

Stamped handles

The makers of spoons with down-turned fiddle-ends between 1820 and 1830 often made plain handles interesting and extremely handsome by stamping decorations on their upper surfaces near the tips. They might add a lobed shell to the die of a French thread-pattern, striking it onto the spoon either on the upper face alone, or on both faces.

King's pattern, which was popular in Great Britain from 1804, and combined threading, a double-swell handle outline, an *anthemion* (flower cluster) and a shell, was adopted by American silversmiths in about 1830. Thomas Fletcher, working in Philadelphia between 1816 and 1841, made 'French forks' (possibly fiddle-end) for $3.40, and 'English forks' (possibly Old English) for $2.25. He also made 'thread and shell' table forks, and 'shell' and 'plain' butter knives. Evans C. Beard of Louisville, Kentucky made 'shell thread' flatwear between 1831 and 1835.

As fortunes grew with the spread of industrialization, the demand for silverware rose markedly. Between 1830 and 1840, therefore, the number of die-sinkers, chasers, ornamental pattern-makers, seal-cutters, engravers, brand- and stamp-cutters increased, each advertising his trade in newspapers and city directories. It took no little skill to cut a pattern with a hard steel tool into a piece of steel, in order to create a die that would stamp so clearly and sharply that there was little need for filing and chasing.

Left to right: Dessert spoon, 1830-40; basket-end downturned fiddle with sugar-loaf shoulders; outlined shell on bowl back; maker's mark: G.C. HOWE/N.Y. with pseudo hall-marks of anchor, bust, star in ovals (George C. Howe, New York, New York); $7\frac{3}{8}$ inches. Dessert spoon, 1825-35; King's pattern single face, outlined shell on bowl back; maker's mark: F.M. and pseudo hall-marks of lion, bust, and G. in rectangles (Frederick Marquand, Savannah, Georgia, 1820-26 and New York, 1824-39); $7\frac{1}{8}$ inches. Dessert spoon, c. 1835; shell-and-thread single-face pattern with pointed shoulders, drop on bowl back, maker's mark B flanked by eagle and Indian in ovals (Theophilus Bradbury 11, Newburyport, Massachusetts); $8\frac{1}{4}$ inches. Tablespoon, c. 1830; King's pattern double face, outlined shell on bowl back; maker's mark: G & M and 2 pseudo hall-marks of bust and eagle in ovals (William Gale and Joseph Moseley, New York, New York); 9 inches. Tablespoon, 1820-30; wheat-end fiddle with rounded shoulders and drop; maker's mark: P MARTIN in rectangle (Peter Martin 11, New York, New York); $8\frac{3}{4}$ inches.

English patterns 1830-60

In the 1830s, several fluidly modelled variations of the fiddle pattern were devised, of which the Albert, Victoria and Devonshire patterns shown here are typical. From the 1840s, a number of new designs more or less based on the fiddle pattern appeared; they were modified either by historicist or naturalistic decoration, both in great demand at the time. Naturalism is represented in the photo by the lily and the palm patterns, and by the christening spoon, with its elaborate leaves and flowers. Tudor, a 19th-century blend of Elizabethan and Jacobean, is exemplified by the Tudor, the 'Ornamental Elizabethan', and the Grecian patterns, and Gothic by New Gothic and Paxton. This last was named in honour of Joseph Paxton, who designed the Crystal Palace for the Great Exhibition of 1851, and it was first shown there. The Napier, outlined with a knotted rope, demonstrates a contemporary striving for originality which sometimes had erratic results.

Most of the spoons illustrated were made as samples for Hunt & Roskell, a London firm, and were not assayed and, therefore, not hallmarked. Francis Higgins and G. W. Adams, some of whose spoons are shown, were probably the most prolific and original English spoonmakers of the second half of the century.

Top, teaspoons, left to right: Elizabethan, London c. 1850; gilt; unmarked. Devonshire or New, London c. 1845; mark only of G.W. Adams. Lily, London, 1850 or later; mark only, of G.W. Adams. Tudor (back), London 1850 or later; mark only, of J.S. Hunt. Napier, London c. 1850; mark only, of J.S. Hunt. 'Ornamental Elizabethan' (back), London 1853; gilt; maker, Francis Higgins. Palm (back), London c. 1850; mark only, of J.S. Hunt.

Bottom, left to right: Teaspoon, Victoria, London 1843; makers, Samuel Hayne and Dudley Cater. Dessert spoon (back), London 1842; gilt; part of christening gift from Queen Victoria to a godchild; makers, Mortimer and Hunt. Dessert spoon, London 1854; makers, Henry Lias I and II; design had appeared by 1840. Teaspoon, Canova, London c. 1850; mark only of G.W. Adams. Tablespoon, Paxton (back), London 1904; maker Elkington and Co.; $8\frac{3}{5}$ inches. Dessert spoon, quilted pattern, London 1895; maker's mark: TS/WS/HH. Dessert spoon, Albert (back), London 1871; maker, Elizabeth Eaton. Dessert spoon, New Gothic, London 1877; maker, G.W. Adams; design registered by Adams 20 November 1852, as 'Elizabethan'.

Patented patterns

Nineteenth-century silversmiths invented their share of labour-saving devices, and as early as 1809 took out patents on them. Some thirty-five years later, on 4 December 1844, the first patent to protect a decorative spoon pattern was filed by Michael Gibney of New York as Design Patent No. 26. This pattern, which was not given a name, added a pointed end and leafy bordering to a double-swell fiddle handle. In 1846 Gibney again filed a patent, this time for a pointed oval-handle pattern he called Olive, which incorporated an oval end, threaded bordering, plain oval reserve and leaf accents. His two innovations encouraged other silversmiths to turn away from the fiddle-ends which had dominated design for fifty years, and led the parade of new patterns that marched through the next fifty. Copies of his Olive pattern with minor changes were called Tuscan or Louis XIV.

The first United States patent law had been enacted in 1790, but had done little to protect the designer's interests, because a patent only lasted three and a half, seven or fourteen years, depending on how large a fee was paid. By changing as little as a leaf or some other minor feature, a competitor could claim a patented design as his own. Gibney's Olive pattern was adopted almost in its entirety by Reed and Barton of Taunton, Massachusetts in 1848, and by Rogers Brothers of Hartford, Connecticut, and William Gale and Sons of New York, in about 1850. It was still being made by three different firms in the 1870s.

Mustard spoon, 1862-65; olive pattern of raised border, reserve, and leafage, double face, on oval, upturned handle; maker's mark: GALE EATON & SNOW (Boston, Massachusetts); 5⅜ inches.

GALE EATON & SNOW

Historicism

There were two approaches to historicism, or the adaptation of past styles in spoon design: direct imitation, which was sometimes indistinguishable from faking, and interpretation. The former began early in the 19th century (travelling spoon, page 46) but was only occasionally used until the wholesale imitation of 18th-century styles began in the 1870s. Interpretation also started during the early years of the century ('rococo' salt spoons, page 90), and was widely practised after 1840, when Germany and Holland became the leading centres for the production of 'Renaissance' and 'medieval' spoons, particularly apostles, which were often struck with false marks. English Arts and Crafts silversmiths frequently returned for inspiration to 16th- and 17th-century English, Dutch or Scandinavian types, as was the case with the Ramsden and Carr spoon shown here, with its 'medieval' figure finial.

Top, left to right: Dessert spoon, London 1880; gilt, set with semi-precious stones; designed by the architect William Burges (1827-81); combination of Roman spoon-shape with stem formed as Gothic column; makers, Barkentin and Krall. Teaspoon, Birmingham 1901; gilt; miniature copy of Coronation Spoon in regalia, made at time of coronation of Edward VII; maker's mark: HFC. Teaspoon, from set, based on Roman spoon; Chester hallmark of 1915; mark of Keswick School of Industrial Arts. Teaspoon, Birmingham 1963; based on Roman spoon; makers, Mappin and Webb. Spoon, German second half of 19th century; parcel-gilt; false mark (a sickle); fanciful combination of Renaissance and later motifs. Spoon (back), probably Austrian c. 1860; gilt and enamelled; from a dessert set; unmarked.

Bottom, left to right: Presentation spoon, London 1916; hexagonal stem and figure knop (figure of Britannia) reflect English 16th-century models; makers, Omar Ramsden and Alwyn Carr. Apostle dessert spoon (St. Thomas), London 1866; parcel-gilt; poor copy of English apostle spoon, en suite with fork; makers, C.T. and G. Fox. Spoon, probably German second half 19th century; parcel-gilt; copy or fake of a Polish or German 16th- or early 17th-century spoon; unmarked; 9 inches. Spoon, German second half 19th century; gilt; Augsburg mark and 13 mark, both probably false; typical of better German spoons in Renaissance style. Apostle spoon (St. Matthew), German second half 19th century; parcel-gilt; false mark (shield of arms); improbable 'medieval' spoon of type also found in pewter. Apostle spoon (St. Matthew), German second half 19th century; gilt, from a set; struck with two false marks; good quality 'early Renaissance' invention.

George Washington medallion

Rarity and historical association have an appeal for the collector, and it follows, therefore, that spoons bearing likenesses of George Washington are in demand. Surprisingly, the first president's image was used very little in flatware until the souvenir-spoon craze of the 1890s. Then his face and form appeared on a dozen or so different handles, produced by as many manufacturers. Among the few examples prior to that are a set, not of spoons, but of forks, with double-swell handles stamped with a laurel border, WASHINGTON, and the head profile. Marked HARLAND (possibly by Henry Harland of New Orleans, Louisiana, who worked in 1831), they may celebrate the hundredth anniversary of Washington's birth in 1732.

At the height of the classic revival, both sculptors and engravers frequently clothed George Washington in a toga and placed him with gods or goddesses in Greek or Roman temples. He was sometimes shown (as in the spoon illustrated) in profile bust in relief, in a classic-style roundel or medallion. This spoon was made in the so-called Age of Elegance—tax-free years when American industrialists built Renaissance, Gothic, French or Venetian palaces and filled them with furniture characterized by panels, arches and heavy mouldings, all derived, by a circuitous route, from the Renaissance.

The spoon itself provides a summary of features peculiar to spoons of the late 19th century: a heart-shaped bowl, less pointed than bowls of the mid-century; a slender stem round in section; a flaring, rounded handle-end. Its decoration, too, exemplifies the era. Derived from Roman medallion busts, or Renaissance revivals of such busts, it includes restrained zigzag bordering which relates to late-18th-century bright-cut bordering.

Teaspoon, 1849; George Washington medallion pattern; maker's mark: N. HARDING & CO/COIN incuse (Boston, Massachusetts); $7\frac{5}{16}$ inches.

American souvenirs

The craze for collecting novel spoons, which reached its height between 1890 and 1910, probably began with travellers venturing far from home on the newly comfortable trains and ships. The first spoon showing a landscape for which the patent is recorded may have touched it all off. Registered in 1881 by Myron H. Kinsley of Wallingford, Connecticut, it depicted the Niagara Falls suspension bridge, a traveller's mecca from 1855 to 1897.

Virtually anything could be pictured in silver or enamel, thanks to a new etching process invented by Reed and Barton's David Howe in about 1900. Spoons with designs appropriate to the occasion were given away in vast numbers, and through souvenir spoons, the unlettered were introduced to famous people, places, flowers, animals and myths.

Clockwise: Souvenir spoon, c. 1890-1900, souvenir of San Francisco; bear of California's seal at handle-tip, shovel and pan commemorating 1849 Gold Rush above grapes signifying vineyards; 'San Francisco' in banner above vine-entwined, beaded stem; 'Cliff House and Seal Rocks, San Francisco' on bowl; on reverse, 'Lucille' in script; maker's mark: SHREVE & CO/STERLING (Shreve & Co., San Francisco, Calif.). Coffee spoon, c. 1890-1902; flowers and leaves engraved on naturalistic handle surrounding 'Lucille'; maker's mark: T ending in anchor entwined with S (Anthony F. Towle & Son Co., Greenfield, Mass.). Souvenir spoon, 1890-1910; Gothic H in wreath with ermine on handle-end; threaded border double-struck; maker's mark: S flanked by lozenges SMITH SILVER^{co} (Frank W. Smith, Gardner, Mass.). Souvenir spoon, 1893, to commemorate World's Columbian Exposition; 'Columbia' with distaff and globe at handle-tip with foliate border; Woman's Building on bowl; on reverse, caravel on waves above exposition's seal and crowned bust of Columbus; foliate stem; maker's mark: 'PAT APPLIED FOR/STERLING' (Alvin manufacturing Co., New York, N.Y.). Coffee spoon, dated 1891; pierced handle with vine, floweret, and tendrils; maker's mark: R.W. & S. STERLING (R. Wallace & Sons Manufacturing Co., Wallingford, Conn.). Souvenir spoon, 1866-1923; handle edged with rococo scrolls; 'LOOKOUT MT.' below picture of mountain on bowl; maker's mark: W/lion/STERLING PAT 1891 (Whitney Manufacturing Co., New York, Bridgeport, Conn. and Providence, R.I.).

American medallions

Naturalistic forms and 18th-century styles were but two of the sources used by designers of spoons between 1860 and 1880. In their search for patterns for mass-production, they frequently chose motifs from the art of past centuries, which they did not hesitate to combine. Many were derived from the Renaissance revival of classic sculpture. Of these, high-relief Roman bust medallions were among the most popular.

Gorham & Company were the first manufacturers to use such a medallion. In 1860 they turned out a spoon whose handle supported a circular frame enclosing the profile bust of a helmeted Roman warrior. During the next few years Hall, Elton & Company of Wallingford, Connecticut; Reed & Barton of Taunton, Massachusetts; Boardman & Son of East Haddam, Connecticut; William B. Durgin of Concord, New Hampshire; W. K. Vanderslice Company of San Francisco, and George W. Shiebler Company of New York used it, or something very similar. Dominick and Haff of New York and Taunton revived it in about 1905.

Roman centurions were displaced by heroes in some medallion patterns. Albert Coles and Company of New York enshrined Sir Walter Scott's Ivanhoe in the classic roundel frame; Newell Harding & Company of Boston memorialized President Washington in much the same way in about 1860.

It was not unusual, in the eclecticism characteristic of design between 1870 and 1890, to employ both a fine Roman head in a Roman medallion and baroque opposing C-scrolls and Gothic tracery. The spoon pictured here typifies this.

Teaspoon, 1860-70; stamped medallion pattern with roundel enclosing helmeted and bearded profile head; the tip of the handle a boss flanked by C-scrolls; the stem Gothic tracery; maker's mark: J & C in two lozenges flanking a circle (unknown); $5\frac{7}{8}$ inches.

Serving and dessert spoons

Serving spoons, simply over-sized tablespoons, were by the 19th century called gravy spoons. The grids in the bowls of some (mainly Irish) and the pierced plates in others, which half cover the bowls, were presumably for straining gravy.

Spoons for serving and eating dessert had broken away from standard patterns by the late 18th century. Throughout the 19th, dessert services were expressions of fantasy and luxury—usually gilt, and heavily ornamented. Among common patterns were the pierced vine which dated from the 1820s, and the solid-stemmed bright vine. The popular vine-and-fruit motif was also used on so-called berry spoons (page 38)—plain 18th-century tablespoons which were later transformed into dessert-serving spoons or fruit spoons by embossing and gilding the bowls and engraving the stems. English spoon bowls were never embellished this way in the 18th century, and the collector should be wary of the genuine hall-marks which the 'improvers' retained. This pernicious practice probably began in the 1820s and is still carried on. New spoons were and are also decorated in the same manner.

Ice spoons originated in the late 18th century and usually had flat-bottomed, spade-like bowls. Solid silver salad servers also appeared in England in the late 18th century, and those with bone handles by 1823. By the 1880s, they were being made with horn, wood, cut-glass or ceramic handles, often *en suite* with salad bowls, as well as in solid silver and electroplate. While a wide range of servers for *hors d'oeuvres* etc. was made in the United States in the late 19th century, the variety in England was more limited.

Top: Gravy spoon, Dublin 1789; double-threaded Old English, removable straining grid; maker, John Dalrymple. Gravy spoon (back), London 1816; stag hunt pattern, stamped with crest and motto of Taylor; maker, Paul Storr.

Bottom, left to right: Ice spade, London 1866; from set with ice spoons; maker, G.W. Adams. Fruit spoon, from cased pair; registered design mark for 9 Sept. 1878; EPNS; bowl once gilt; design at top derived from ferns and spores; angularity of form characteristic of 1860s and 1870s. Ice cream spoon, (?) German or Austrian c. 1880-1900; silver, frosted and gilt, in case with knife; marked '800' and 's' below unidentifiable symbol; bowl bright-cut engraved in Japanese taste. Server, Sheffield 1908; perhaps for hors-d'oeuvres; 'bowl' very shallow; maker, Henry Archer and Co.

Ladles and sugar sifters

Soup and sauce ladles designed by size for their purposes first appeared on the Continent in the mid-18th century, but were rare in English silver until the 1760s. At the same time, the Old English stem and round bowl were adopted. Thereafter, standard stem shapes were employed, and the bowls of many ladles after 1800 were oval. Sugar sifters originated in about 1750, and although they were at first small in England (about five inches), by 1800 they had become the size of sauce ladles. They were then also often given round, flat-bottomed bowls.

From the 1840s, sugar sifters and dessert ladles were frequently treated as 'fancy spoons' and made in a wide variety of shapes, many of them naturalistic, the spoon stem being formed as a plant stem and the bowl as a flower or leaf. The ladle shown here (designed by Dr. Christopher Dresser, one of the founders of modern functional design) is a remarkable anticipation of 20th-century forms.

Punch ladles originated in the late 17th century. Those with whalebone handles, so commonly seen, began in about 1760 and were made all over Europe well into the 19th century. Their bowls are often very thin, and English examples, many unmarked, were frequently beaten out of coins with the inscriptions showing on their rims, as in the illustration. Continental bowls tend to have pronounced pouring lips. The smaller toddy ladle, which appeared in England in about 1800, was particularly popular in Scotland (page 50).

Top, left to right: Sauce ladle, London c. 1760; Hanoverian; engraved with royal arms and GR; maker's mark: IT. Sugar sifter, London 1790; Old English; maker, probably Hester Bateman. Punch ladle, English c. 1800; twisted whalebone handle; unmarked; 14⅖ inches. Sugar sifter, Norwegian (Bergen) 1857; parcel-gilt; fiddle pattern, applied shell; maker, Nicolai Monclair. Sauce ladle, London 1827; Coburg pattern; maker, William Chawner II.

Bottom, left to right: Sauce ladle, London 1909; 'planished' finish to spoon; makers, Omar Ramsden and Alwyn Carr. Sauce ladle, German, c. 1905; double-struck stem; maker's mark: (?) a torch. Dessert ladle, English c. 1970; King's pattern; stamped EPNS; gilt bowl; poorly-made version of 19th-century design. Sauce (or cream) ladle, Exeter 1846; maker, W.R. Sobey. Sauce ladle, Danish (Copenhagen) c. 1929; 'planished'; based on Scandinavian 17th-century spoons; designer, Georg Jensen, probably 1909; London import marks for 1929; maker, Jensen. (Below) soup ladle, Birmingham 1880 or later; electro-plated; ebony handle; designer, Dr Christopher Dresser (1834-1904); design registration mark, 28 July 1880; en suite with tureen; makers, Hukin and Heath.

American varieties

American households at the beginning of the 19th century owned a satisfactory variety of eating utensils held over from the 18th century. A knife and a tablespoon for each diner had been the rule as early as the start of the 18th, with possibly a dinner fork for adults and a sweetmeat fork or two, if the household was a wealthy one.

As the 18th century advanced, the repertoire of silversmiths grew larger and more varied. They made small spoons to fit the cups of Chinese fashion that held the new 'China drink', 'cream spoons' of a medium size that would go deep into jelly- and syllabub-glasses and cream cups, and large spoons to serve the essence from roasts, which were customarily carved on platters by diners at the table. They also fashioned salt shovels (later termed salt ladles and later still, salt spoons), which did away with the use of knives as conveyors of salt. By the time the century was half gone, they were specializing even further, with spoons designed expressly for such purposes as eating boiled eggs from the shell or transferring tea leaves from the tea caddy to the pot.

Today's canny collector may find 18th- and 19th-century English caddy spoons or caddy shells made of silver, tortoise-shell, mother-of-pearl, bone, ivory, agate, wood or earthenware, but he will be extremely lucky to find one of the few remaining American examples of either century.

Left to right: Sugar sifter, c. 1859; olive pattern, double-struck; maker's mark: FREEMAN & BENNETT, Patent 1859, in incised capitals (New York, New York); $7\frac{9}{16}$ inches. Caddy shell, 1780-90; scallop-shell bowl, polygonal flat handle, roulette-line border; maker's mark: I. LOWNES in script (Joseph Lownes, Philadelphia, Pennsylvania); $2\frac{15}{16}$ inches. Gravy spoon, 1820-29; rounded, downturned, with vestigial midrib on back; modelled pointed-arch drop on bowl back; maker's mark: SHEPHERD & BOYD in rectangle (Robert Shepherd and William Boyd, Albany, New York) $13\frac{3}{8}$ inches.

Above, left to right: Miniature ladle, 1820-40; downturned fiddle-end, flaring shoulders; no maker's mark; $2\frac{5}{16}$ inches. Miniature teaspoon, c. 1845; double-swell fiddle-handle; maker's mark: CROSBY & BROWN (Samuel T. Crosby and Seth E. Brown, Boston, Massachusetts); $3\frac{3}{4}$ inches. Salt shovel, c. 1860; upturned fiddle-end, rounded flaring shoulders; maker's mark: F. BROWN & CO in rectangle (Francis Brown and S. W. Marsters, New York, New York); $3\frac{7}{8}$ inches. Egg spoon, c. 1835; fiddle-thread pattern, upturned; gilt, fig-shaped bowl; maker's mark: GELSTON in rectangle (George S. Gelston, New York, New York); $4\frac{1}{2}$ inches.

English patterns 1860-1900

The only 19th-century pattern to join the standard English repertory after 1860 was the Albany, which had appeared by the mid-1880s, and was perhaps named after Queen Victoria's youngest son, the Duke of Albany, who died in 1884. It is described as 'Queen Anne' in a Higgins catalogue and, with its slender stem and delicate linear decoration, shows the revived interest in 18th-century styles which had begun in the 1860s. Old English, which had never ceased to be made, gradually became more sought after and eventually usurped the fiddle's premier position. There was also a revival of bright-cut engraving and of copies of trifid, wavy-ended and Onslow spoons.

At the same time, designs with classical overtones based on French Empire originals appeared. Typical are the 'fish and game' pattern and the graceful teaspoon of 1881 shown here. From the 1870s, there was a movement towards patterns derived from Japanese art, most commonly expressed by asymmetrical representations of birds and foliage stamped onto bowls and stems of standard shape. The fruit spoon illustrated, a strange blend of Japanese and less frequently used Egyptian motifs, is characteristic of the period from about 1870 to 1920 when many novel, short-lived designs were applied to servers and to dessert, tea, coffee, condiment and christening spoons.

Top, left to right: Dessert spoon, Japanese c. 1900; bamboo-shaped stem; marked 'Musashiya' in Japanese characters; such spoons were copied in Europe. Child's spoon, London 1883; bright-cut; from christening set with knife, fork, napkin ring; maker, G.M. Jackson. Dessert spoon, Dublin 1865; bright-cut fiddle; maker, (?) J. Smyth. Teaspoon, London 1872; fish and game pattern; mark of Hunt and Roskell. Two teaspoons, London c. 1870 and 1860; marks of Hunt and Roskell and J.S. Hunt.

Bottom, left to right: Teaspoon (back), (?), Italian c. 1880; electro-plated; unmarked. Japanese-inspired design on bowl; $7\frac{1}{5}$ inches. Teaspoon, London 1871; gilt; maker, Francis Higgins. Teaspoon, London 1881; maker, G.W. Adams. Teaspoon, London (Britannia standard marks) 1903; trifid pattern ('James I' in a Higgins pattern book); bowl stamped with relief decoration; maker, Thomas Bradbury. Fruit spoon, Sheffield 1872 or later; EPNS; one of pair, in case marked Mappin and Webb, design registered 26 October 1872; maker, W.H. & Co. Four teaspoons: beaded Old English, London c. 1850, mark of J.S. Hunt; plain Old English, London 1845, maker, G.W. Adams; wavy end ('trefoil rat-tail' in a Higgins catalogue), London c. 1880, maker, Francis Higgins; threaded Old English, London c. 1850, maker, G.W. Adams; (below) ice-spade, London 1898; Albany; maker, Francis Higgins.

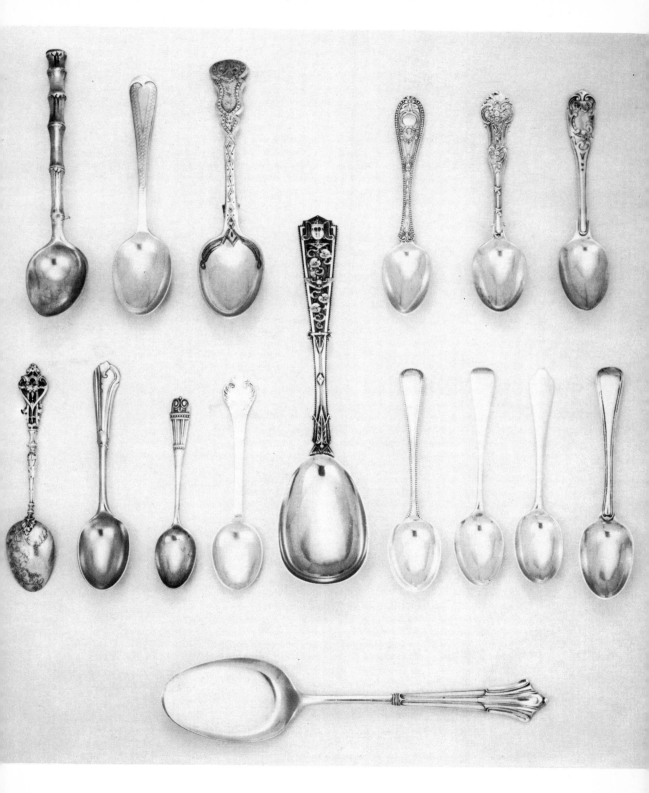

European souvenirs

Spoons to commemorate special occasions have been made for the last three centuries. Christening spoons date from the 16th, and those connected with national events from the 17th. The 'picture-back' bowl decoration of the 18th century was frequently political (page 86), and English spoonmakers in the 19th century made cheap spoons for the American and French markets with political emblems on the stems.

The modern souvenir spoon, in which the emblem dominates the stem, had appeared by 1843, when a design was registered with the Prince of Wales' triple plume in silhouette. By the 1880s, the British were making spoons as souvenirs of places, some for home consumption, many for export (see also page 70). At about the same time, the English began to manufacture spoons for sports and competition prizes. Good design need not necessarily be absent, as the illustrations on pages 99 and 105 show.

Top, left to right: Coffee spoon, Maltese, after 1920; souvenir, Malta; maker, A. Michele Michaleff. Coffee spoon, souvenir, Scotland; Edinburgh 1929. Coffee spoon, German c. 1900 or later; EPNS; shield on stem blank to be enamelled; marked ALPACCA VERSILBERT.

Middle, left to right: Coronation teaspoon (George VI), Sheffield 1937; stem engraved with crown and laurel wreath, bowl stamped with ship; copy of 18th-century 'picture-back'; maker, Thomas Bradbury & Sons. Golf-prize teaspoon, Birmingham 1936; initials WNGA on stem; maker's mark: BBS Ltd. Cricket-prize teaspoon, Birmingham 1928; 9 ct. gold; design registered 1902; maker's mark: AF (?). Cricket-prize teaspoon, Sheffield 1931; initials, FMCC on stem; maker, C.W. Fletcher & Sons. Coronation coffee spoon, from set, London 1952; in bowl, coronation mark (crowned head of Elizabeth II) used from May 1952 to May 1954; maker's mark: RWB.

Bottom, left to right: Sugar spoon, Birmingham 1907; enamelled; souvenir, Franco-British Exhibition, London 1908; makers, Elkington & Co. Sugar sifter, EPNS, enamelled; souvenir, North East Coast Exhibition, Newcastle-upon-Tyne, 1929; maker unknown; $5\frac{1}{10}$ inches. Spoon, modern Norwegian; silver-gilt and enamel; souvenir, Oslo with city's arms; maker, David-Andersen, Oslo.

Specialized varieties

There has always been tremendous ingenuity in spoon-invention to cope with specialized needs. Medicine spoons, for instance, have been made since the 16th century in many materials and miniatures of adults' spoons, probably designed for children, began to appear in the 15th. Marrow scoops, used to extract marrow from beef bones, formed part of dinner services from about 1700 to 1900. Recognizable caddy spoons date from 1770. From about 1850, children's spoons were commonly made as christening presents in cased sets (page 80). Fruit, preserve and round-bowled soup spoons all appeared in the late Victorian era. Dessert spoons had come in the mid-18th century (page 74). The type shown here, with a handle of silver, ivory or mother-of-pearl, probably originated in the 1840s. The precise purpose of the 18th-century 'mote spoon' (page 38), which was made in several sizes, is obscure, but the teaspoon-sized examples may have been used for straining tea.

Top, left to right: Dessert spoon, Birmingham 1858; en suite *with fork; handle separately made of thin silver; makers, Hilliard and Thomason. Orange or grapefruit spoon, Sheffield 1935; maker, A.E. Poston and Co. Honey spoon, Sheffield 1935; hook at back of stem; design still made; makers, Roberts and Belk. (?) Porridge spoon, Sheffield 1903 or later; EPNS; maker's mark:* R & S; *design registered 1903 by Robinson & Sons, oatmeal manufacturers. Jam spoon, Birmingham 1913; Belmont II pattern; maker's mark:* W.H.H. *Preserve spoon, Swedish c. 1900; EPNS; stamped* ALP. NS. *Jam spoon, English c. 1870-1900; EPNS.*

Bottom, left to right: Ice spoon, Sheffield c. 1900 or later; EPNS; makers, Mappin and Webb. Sugar spoon, London 1879; maker, G.W. Adams. Chutney fork, London 1875; Grecian pattern; maker, G.W. Adams; pattern registered 19 September 1851; shown at Great Exhibition. Child's spoon, Sheffield 1924 or later; en suite *with a bowl; EPNS; makers, Harrison Brothers and Howson (Reg. design no. 708938). Medicine spoon, Exeter 1859; bowl of tablespoon size; maker, John Stone. Travelling or medicine spoon, London 1875; larger bowl is size of large teaspoon; maker, G.W. Adams. Sugar scoop, Norwegian (Bergen) 1858; maker, A.C. Møgelvang.*
Below: Child's spoon, Sheffield 1930 or later; looped stem, EPNS; marked DUCHESS PLATE *(Reg. design no. 758470); type described 'As used in the United States' in English catalogue c. 1905. Caddy spoon, Birmingham c. 1904 or later; pewter; originally designed by Rex Silver for Liberty and Co., London; stamped* MADE IN ENGLAND/ SOLKETS/ENGLISH PEWTER/01242; *maker, W. H. Haseler. Below: Marrow scoop, London 1780; maker, George Smith III.*

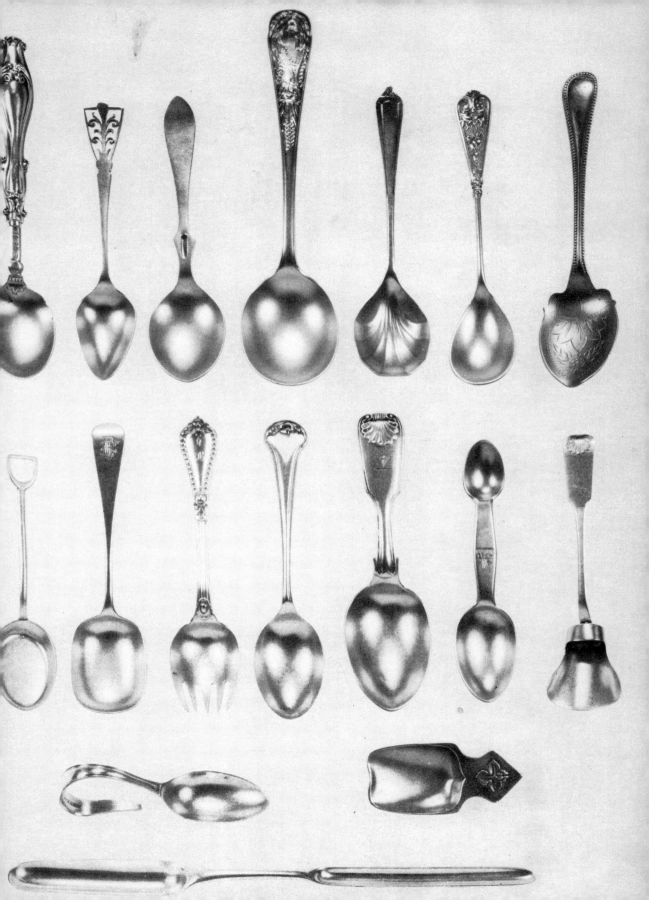

Tea, coffee, egg and miniature spoons

Tea and coffee spoons were both first made in the late 17th century, but appear to have been indistinguishable until the late 19th century, when they were first separately listed in catalogues. Before then, they were called teaspoons in tea-drinking countries, and coffee spoons in coffee-drinking. English spoons were small and light until about 1800 when, under French influence, they became very large. From about 1870 there was again a general reduction in size, which produced the 'afternoon teaspoon'—light and often fanciful. Coffee spoons were made in many forms, all small and delicate and frequently gilt; the smallest are called mocha spoons.

Spoons designed with long bowls for eating eggs—often gilded to prevent staining—appeared in England in the late 18th century; shield-shaped bowls came a little later. Miniature spoons, now called snuff spoons, had various unspecified uses, and were sometimes included in travelling sets and *étuis*; many were toys. Small EPNS spoons are described as 'for children's tea sets' in an 1889 catalogue.

Top, teaspoons, left to right:|Hanoverian, London c. 1760; maker's mark: WW. \Old English, London 1807; makers, William Eley and William Fearn.\ Old English (back), London c. 1770; design stamped on bowl: bird released from cage, 'I Love Liberty' inscribed above, commemorating release of John Wilkes (1727-97) from prison (page 82); maker, Phillip Roker. \Fiddle pattern (back), Sheffield c. 1850-1900; EPNS; makers, Daniel and Arter.I Bright-cut Old English, London 1898; makers, Wakely and Wheeler; $4\frac{7}{10}$ inches. Afternoon teaspoon, Sheffield 1915; 'Seal-top' design; maker's mark: PHA in script. Afternoon teaspoon, London 1896; apostle; from cased set with sugar tongs; makers, W. Hutton and Sons Ltd. Unidentified pattern, Birmingham 1925 or later; EPNS.

Centre, left to right: Egg spoon, (?) Birmingham c. 1840; (?) close-plated nickel-silver; maker's mark: BURTON. Miniature spoons: toy ladle, Dutch 18th or 19th century; London c. 1760, maker, Ebenezer Coker; London 1799, from cased set with tongs, maker, George Smith; Exeter 1824, maker, Joseph Hicks. Egg spoon, London 1833.

Bottom, coffee spoons, left to right: Enamelled silver-gilt; Birmingham 1937; maker's mark: T & S. Flowered stem, Swedish (Malmö) 1970; maker's mark: GEWE. Gilt base-metal, c. 1900; unmarked. Gilt copper; Swedish c. 1935; unmarked. Silver-gilt, German (? Hamburg) c. 1905; Art Nouveau stem. Silver-gilt, German (? Cassel), c. 1905 Jugendstil stem. 'Bean spoon', Sheffield 1937; type introduced in late 19th century; maker's mark: E W. 'Adam revival' stem, London, 1919; maker's mark illegible. Above, horizontal (back): Birmingham 1920; enamelled silver-gilt; maker's mark: S LIMITED.

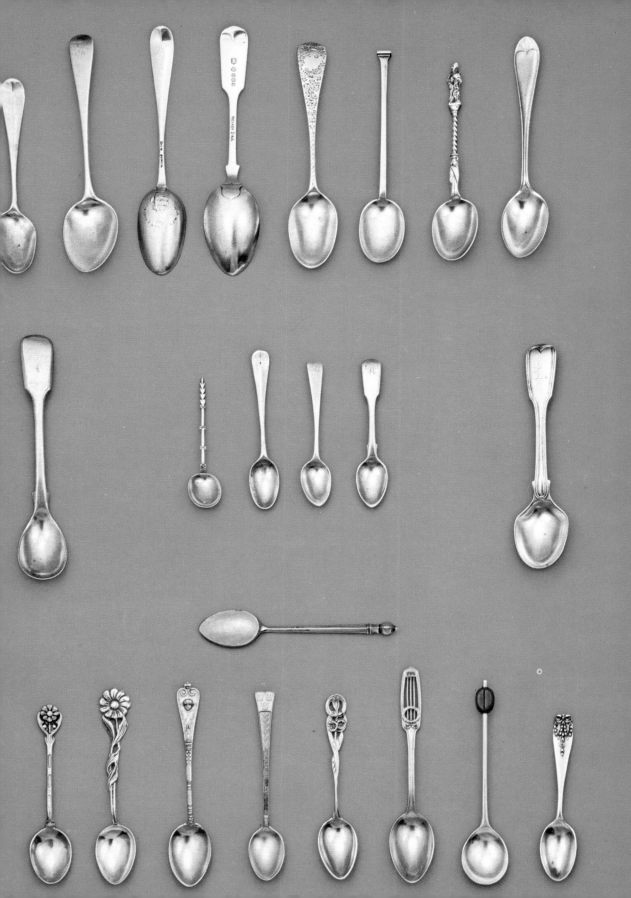

Egg spoons and gilding

Hugh Thompson, Esq. of Baltimore bought from Rundell and Bridge, Jewellers and Goldsmiths, a 'Plated egg Frame and Cups gilt inside with Spoons £3.10.0 2 Feb. 1797'. This was a rare purchase, for American silversmiths in the 18th century seldom made egg spoons. By the middle of the 19th century, however, they were considered a necessary part of flatware services. Egg spoons in sets of four, six, eight or twelve were sold with as many egg cups held in a stand, or frame.

Never much more than four and one-half inches long overall, the spoons usually—and very properly—had egg-shaped bowls. But sometimes the bowls were rounded and the handles elaborately embellished, as in the spoon pictured here. Employing Gothic arches on a spoon intended for the eating of soft-boiled eggs seems absurd, but it is not more absurd in its relation of use to decoration than were many other spoons of the 19th century. Absurdity in this case is redeemed by the well-proportioned design elements, by the careful chasing of arches, crockets, quatrefoil and colonnettes of the handle and by the simple threaded and leaf-accented stem above a pleasingly rounded gilded bowl.

The bowls of egg spoons, like those of salt, sugar, ice-cream, berry, pickle, olive and mustard spoons, were customarily gilded. In the 18th century this had been accomplished by fire-gilding, dissolving gold in mercury and spreading it on silver objects. Heated in a fire, the mercury evaporated leaving the gold fused to the silver. But the process was abandoned early in the 19th century because the mercury fumes were poisonous to workers. Electrolysis instead became the method, following experiments by Rundell's in about 1805 and patents by Elkington's in 1836 and 1840. The new technique, which placed a satisfactory film of gold on a spoon bowl, is still in use, and produces a gold deeper in colour than the earlier mercury gilding.

Egg spoon, 1855-65; stamped Gothic pattern; a quatrefoil in a pointed arch edged with crockets, above a double pointed arch, supported by colonnettes; threaded stem with leaf accents; gilt round/oval bowl; maker's mark: WM. GALE & SON/925/STERLING incuse (New York, New York,); $4\frac{7}{16}$ inches.

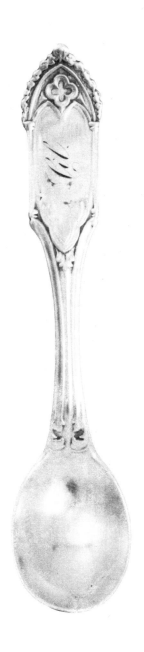

Condiment spoons and small ladles

Small, specialized ladles for sugar, pepper, mustard and cream began to be made in England in the mid-18th century. Most examples, however, date only from after 1770 and used standard stem types. Pepper ladles (included in cruet sets) died out after 1800, but mustard and cream ladles (sometimes indistinguishable) continued, as did mustard spoons. The earliest surviving undecorated salt spoons have shovel-shaped bowls and date from the mid-18th century. After 1770 the Old English stem was adopted, and remained in use for plain salt spoons until after 1900. Salt spoons have been made in fanciful forms since the 1740s, when the 'whiplash' stem was introduced. During the following century, historicist and other novel designs grew popular, particularly from about 1840; coincidentally, the spoons became smaller. The type frequently seen with a wire stem that terminates in a ball dates from the late 19th century.

Top, left to right: (?) Cream ladle, London 1790; maker, Hester Bateman. Long mustard ladle, London 1847; maker, G.W. Adams. (?) Pepper ladle, London c. 1765 (piercing may be later); scroll-ended Onslow stem; maker's mark: I I. Pepper ladle, London 1792; makers, George Smith and William Fearn. Mustard spoon, London 1795; makers, as above. Mustard ladle, London 1833; King's husk pattern; (?) maker, Joseph Wintle. Mustard spoon, London 1901; set with a chrysoprase; designer, C.R. Ashbee; maker, Guild of Handicraft Ltd.

Middle, salt spoons, left to right: London c. 1750; maker's mark illegible. English late 18th century; 'whiplash' stem; unmarked. London 1840; bright-cut stem; maker's mark illegible. London probably c. 1761; from plate of Queen Charlotte, consort of George III; contemporary interpretation of French fiddle pattern; unmarked, but perhaps by Thomas Heming; 4½ inches. London 1812; maker, Thomas Holland. Sheffield 1819; inspired by 18th-century rococo spoons; maker, Robert Gainsford. London 1843; also rococo.

Bottom, mainly salt spoons, left to right: Mustard spoon, London 1878; design dates from at least 1844; for use with owl-shaped mustard pots; mouse appears to hang from bird's beak when pot is closed; maker, G.W. Adams. London 1843; stem of German 16th-century type; maker, Robert Garrard. Sheffield 1880; historicist use of 'maidenhead' finial; maker, Martin Hall and Co. London 1862; maker's mark illegible. Pewter, English 19th century; unmarked. Danish (Copenhagen) c. 1926; from Acanthus pattern service; designer, Johan Rohde, 1917; maker, Georg Jensen. London 1911; maker's mark: WB. German c. 1920; enamelled silver-gilt. EPNS Sheffield 1933, or later (Reg. design no. 780234); makers, Walker and Hall. Swedish (Gothenburg) 1952; based on a Lapp spoon design. London 1900; designer, C.R. Ashbee; set with a chrysoprase.

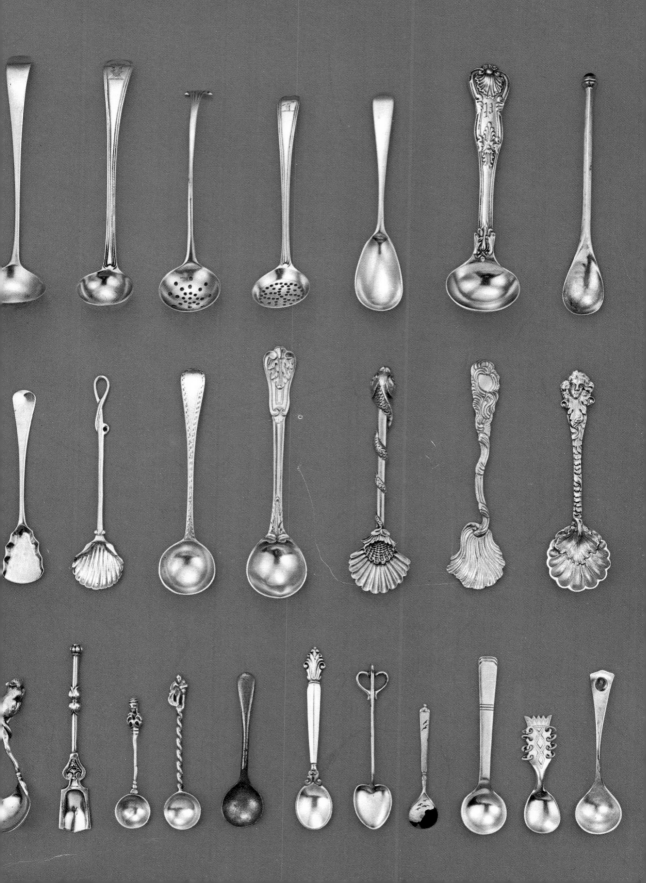

New spoon forms

A phenomenon of the 19th century was the enormous proliferation of flatware forms. Designers sketched new implements by the dozen. There were few foods for which special serving and/or eating tools were not created. Of spoons especially, at least three dozen kinds existed, from berry spoons and orange spoons to macaroni, pea, piccalilli and claret spoons. The Towle Manufacturing Company alone put out in 1905 thirty-five different spoon forms in every one of their patterns. These excluded ladles, of which there were some dozen.

In addition to specialized spoons manufactured to match flatware services, there were numerous other spoons, each bearing some ingenious feature which fitted it to serve a specific purpose. One medicine spoon bore a dial and hands on its handle; a second had a curved handle, and a bowl bent into a tube to insert between the lips. A moustache spoon had a shield on one side to hold the moustache away from the food. A birthday spoon was decorated with the twelve birth-flowers and the signs of the zodiac. A child's spoon was bordered by animals. All were patented.

Of the three dozen or so forms included with every full 19th-century service of flatware, only nine are made today without special order. One of the all but forgotten specialized shapes that rocketed to its zenith in the 1880s and faded out soon afterwards was the berry spoon. No longer generally made, it yet survives in many patterns to provide haunters of curio shops with an 'antique' to give as a wedding present.

Berry spoon, 1860-70; pointed oval downturned handle with oval reserve, pendent bowknot and husks; heart-shaped bowl with raised midrib and scallop flanges; bowl bright-engraved with tendrils and flowerets; evidence of gold wash; maker's mark: L. LADOMUS & Co./STERLING incuse (Lewis Ladomus and H. Bulon, Philadelphia, Pennsylvania); $9\frac{3}{4}$ inches.

STERLING   L. LADOMUS & Cᵒ.

Flower patterns

In the opulent 1880s there was a whirlwind of ideas for ornamenting flatware, ranging from the extravagantly florid to the extremely simple. If a collector were to search for spoons that typified the design of the period, he would have to choose between flamboyant patterns that covered, or all but covered, a multi-curved handle, and quiet patterns that accented a handle of plain background and straight lines.

Many of the former were derived from flowers, which were interpreted in countless ways. The most popular expressions were in the highly imaginative, romantic manner that had survived from earlier in the century. A few, like Wood & Hughes' Marguerite, first made in about 1880, exemplified the classical revival which ran concurrently with the taste for the lavish in the late 19th century. The marguerite, a simple and orderly flower, has in the pattern been arranged around a pseudo-classical shield flanked with garlands tied with a bowknot. The neat, restrained design is stamped onto a handle whose outlines disdain the rococo curves that dominated the flatware of the decade and had done so since the 1860s.

When the Gorham Manufacturing Company, in about 1881, issued a pattern also called Marguerite, it combined both trends. The outlines were unbroken, as in Old English spoons of the 1780s, but the design presented the flower in an asymmetrical, naturalistic manner around a formless reserve, making the whole decidedly undistinguished. Gorham issued a New Marguerite in 1901, equally indifferent, with a double-swell outline and naturalistic flowers whose leaves were treated as if they were rococo scrolls surrounding the reserve.

Teaspoon, 1880-90; Marguerite pattern; maker's mark: Ww H (Jacob Wood and Jasper W. Hughes, New York, mark used 1871-99); dealer's mark: COOK and JAQUES (location unknown); 7$\frac{5}{16}$ inches.

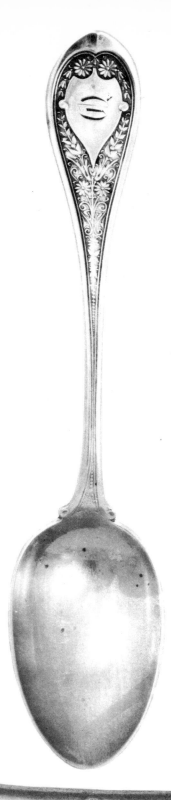

French-style American spoons

In the 1890s, when French chateaux were rising in American cities, fashionable Francophiles chose silver patterns with such evocative names as *La Reine, l'Elégante*; and *Chambord.* Duhme and Company (1837-87), called The Tiffany of the West, in catering to Ohio's finest families from its seat in Cincinnati on the Ohio River, sold both stamped and hand-engraved spoons in 'French' patterns. Later, as the Duhme Jewelry Company (from about 1887-1907), they engaged in design-copying, and used the scrolled pattern that Reed & Barton had patented on 7 March, 1897 under the name *La Comtesse.* The Duhme & Company pattern on the sugar shell pictured is related in its balanced engraving, wrigglework border, twist handle and pointed shoulders to the 1867 Twist Engraved pattern of Joseph Seymour Sons & Company, Syracuse, New York (worked from 1835 to about 1900).

Like other silver manufacturing and marketing firms, Duhme offered special pieces of flatware individually, with dinner services or in presentation sets. These last consisted of such combinations as a soup set of one ladle and six spoons; a chocolate set of one muddler (a long spoon) and six round spoons; a coffee set of tongs and six oval spoons; a tea set of butter knife, sugar shell and six teaspoons, or an ice-cream set of one ice-cream knife and six ice-cream spoons. Boxed and labelled, such assemblages made much-admired gifts.

Sugar shell, 1880-85; engraved open design of stylized leaves and roulette-bordered handle above twisted stem; maker's mark: DUHME & CO in cartouche, STERLING 925/1000 (Cincinnati, Ohio); $6\frac{5}{16}$ inches.

Art Nouveau, Arts and Crafts, and Jugendstil

The English Arts and Crafts movement, Art Nouveau in France and Jugendstil in Germany all attempted, during the late 19th and early 20th centuries, to create a new type of design not directly imitative of historical styles. William Morris and his Arts and Crafts group were, of course, in the vanguard in England, but organizations such as C. R. Ashbee's Guild of Handicraft and the Keswick School of Industrial Arts also rejected machine-production and used only hand manufacture. Although most Arts and Crafts spoons derive loosely from historical patterns, they usually bear visible hammer marks and are often set with enamels or semi-precious stones. Art Nouveau and early Jugendstil used a sinuous plant-like line for the stem (also in U.S., page 100), but the bowl was usually conventional. By about 1900 Jugendstil had become angular and geometric; the spoon shown here is a restrained example.

From about 1900, the London store, Liberty and Co., produced its own range of silver and pewter wares, including numerous distinctive spoons which combined Art Nouveau and Arts and Crafts styles, but were nevertheless made almost entirely by machine. Some of the most beautiful spoons of the period—Scandinavian Art Nouveau based on vegetable forms—came from the Copenhagen firm of Georg Jensen, which continues still to make several early patterns.

Top row, left to right: Tea or coffee spoon, Danish (Copenhagen) c. 1929; 'beaded' pattern; London import marks for 1929; $4\frac{7}{10}$ inches. Tea or coffee spoon, Swedish c. 1905 or later; EPNS; bowl gilt; marked PRIMA NS 1. Spoon, Birmingham 1901; enamelled silver; mark of Liberty and Co. (Cymric) Ltd; designer, Archibald Knox (1864-1933); maker, W.H. Haseler Ltd; the type was reproduced for coronation of George V, 1910. Teaspoon, Sheffield 1912, from set; maker, W. Hutton & Sons. Tea or coffee spoon, London 1901; silver set with stained chalcedony, imitating chrysoprase; designer, C.R. Ashbee (1863-1942). Teaspoon, from set of six; differing finials connected with legend of St Columba; Chester hall-mark for 1917.

Bottom row, left to right: Tea or coffee spoon, Danish (Copenhagen) 1908; 'Viking' style; maker, VM; $4\frac{8}{10}$ inches. Coffee spoon, Danish (Copenhagen) 1922; maker, Georg Jensen; London import marks for 1922. Jam or dessert spoon, German c. 1910; bowl gilt; Jugendstil stem; maker's mark: P.J. and an arrow. Serving spoon, Danish (Copenhagen) 1926; designer and maker, Georg Jensen. Teaspoon, Birmingham 1902; from set in Liberty and Co's 'Adela' pattern dating from 1899. Christening spoon, English 1909; child's face surrounded by stars at top of stem; no marks; Arts and Crafts designer-maker, John Paul Cooper (1869-1933). Egg spoon, Birmingham 1914; mark of designer-maker, John Paul Cooper.

Turn of the century

From the third quarter of the 18th century, when the Birmingham and Sheffield metal trades had first broken large jobs down into small ones, stamped small objects out by the thousands and produced 'spoons struck at once', as Dr Johnson put it in 1774, 'machine-made' had meant, for the average householder, dependable quality at reasonable prices. However, in the haste of the division of labour, of mass production and the use of power tools, bad design, often lifeless and unoriginal, had swept over domestic articles. By the end of the 19th century numerous people reacted against it, and advocated a back-to-the-hand movement.

The linear, asymmetrical styles, largely derived from plant life, which came to be called Art Nouveau, and were instigated in England by William Morris, among others (see page 98), were also well received in the United States. Some of them were chased handsomely onto silver by such firms as Unger Brothers, Newark and New York, and by Tiffany & Company, New York; many went onto plated silver.

Happily, the new design was also reflected in stamped flatware patterns. While well-to-do Americans at the turn of the century could buy hand-wrought place settings, each piece adorned with a different Japanese bird or reed, the less affluent could buy sets of twelve stamped spoons, each bearing a different flower. Such series, showing a variety of realistic blossoms instead of one repeated conventionalized bloom, were introduced between 1900 and 1910 by a dozen or more American silver manufacturers. To be sure, their designs were more sculptural than linear, but they were organic and asymmetrical and made use of the plastic quality of silver in a satisfactory way.

Teaspoon, c. 1906; Columbine pattern, naturalistic blossom with leaves and buds; double face; ribbon and bowknot, seed-pod and leaves on reverse; maker's mark: RW/&S flanking an antlered head /STERLING (R. Wallace and Sons Manufacturing Company, Wallingford, Connecticut, 1871-1955, now Wallace Silversmiths); 5⅞ inches.

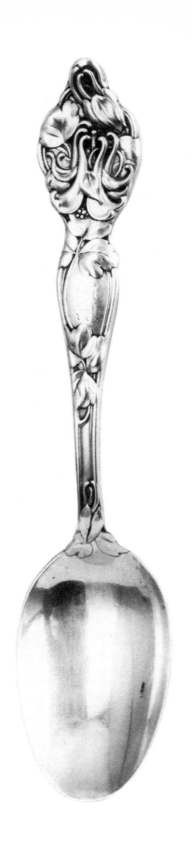

Tiffany and Company

Charles L. Tiffany was a partner in Tiffany & Young of New York between 1837 and 1848. The firm sold silver made by John Moore, New York, who had been a silversmith since 1827. With Moore as partner, Tiffany formed a company in 1853, which, 125 years later, is one of the foremost American silver firms and among a dozen which have been in operation since the 18th or early 19th century. Always respected for the quality of its silver and jewellery, Tiffany and Company in about 1902 produced a berry spoon of great weight, good balance and fine workmanship. The hitherto unpublished mark, TIFFANY & CO./MAKERS/STERLING, was cut into the die for the spoon's back, together with berries, blossoms and leaves.

The mark and pattern were both raised at the same time, and stand as an early example of the simultaneous cutting, decorating and making that in the 20th century supplanted the separate striking of an intaglio, or incuse mark. Such pieces were typical of the turn of the century. Although life was accelerating with the invention of the automobile, the aeroplane, the transatlantic cable and the lift (elevator), society still sat through meals of five to ten courses, and their tables were arrayed with eating implements in serried ranks and with serving tools in clusters. Serving pieces usually matched the main service, but some had specially designed handles.

Tiffany's berry spoon formed part of no known set. Nor was it related either to Georgian and other post-centennial 'colonial' designs, or to such patterns as Warwick, Westminster and Countess, which reflected the contemporaneous interest in marriages between American money and British titles. It was, however, in the mood of *La Vigne, La Grappe,* Vintage and Vine, all patterns with which silver and electroplate manufacturers between 1900 and 1910 celebrated the grape.

Berry spoon, c. 1902; asymmetrical fig-shaped bowl; double-struck heavy and thick handle of berry, blossom and leaf design; maker's mark: TIFFANY & CO./MAKERS/STERLING raised on reserve on back.

British and European spoons, 1920-50

English spoon-design between 1920 and 1950 was in general exceedingly conservative. The spoons shown here by Omar Ramsden and Bernard Cuzner, who were among the most important English silversmiths of their day, are typical of the later spoons in the Arts and Crafts tradition, which survived in England until the 1940s. Commercial English patterns after 1900 were often weakly conceived versions of French Empire and 'Louis XVI' styles, and betray their modernity only by their increasingly simplified forms. The angularities of the French fashion of the 1920s and 1930s, now known as 'art deco', arrived in England rather late, and then tended to be imposed on existing forms, as was the case with the Gloucester pattern (opposite), which is 'updated' by a chevron design stamped on its stem. It is described in a contemporary catalogue as one of Elkington and Co.'s 'latest and most exclusive patterns illustrating the modern trend in silverware'.

The spoon shown here by Jean Puiforcat, the leading French silversmith of the 1920s and 1930s, is, with its round bowl and wide flat stem, typical of French 'art deco' spoons. The spoons by Joyce Himsworth, who worked in Sheffield, were influenced by such French models. 'Art deco' spoons were sometimes so stylistically formalised as to become almost useless. The Jensen scoop illustrated is a practical version of a stylized French design. In Germany and Scandinavia, plain and functional spoons, which were to have a considerable influence later, had been made since the early years of the century.

Top, left to right: Tablespoon, Birmingham 1935; Gloucester pattern; stamped chevron design, registered 1928; maker, Elkington & Co. Three small spoons, Sheffield 1936; niello decoration on stems; one a coronation spoon; designer and maker, Joyce Himsworth. Serving spoon, London 1933; maker, Omar Ramsden (1873-1939).

Centre: Souvenir spoon of Paris Exhibition, 1937; maker's mark of Jean Puiforcat, Paris.

Bottom, left to right: Scoop, Danish (Copenhagen) c. 1930; pyramid pattern; stem hollow; designed for Jensen by Harald Nielsen, 1927; London import marks for 1930; maker, Georg Jensen; $5\frac{9}{10}$ inches. Dessert spoon, Birmingham 1927; illustrated in Studio Year Book, *1929; designer and maker, Bernard Cuzner (1877-1956). Child's combined spoon and fork, Swedish c. 1943; EPNS; marked* GABEX. P. NS. ALP.

Spoons after 1950

The modern clean-lined functional spoon represents the greatest advance in design since the medieval and Renaissance thin-stemmed spoon was abandoned for the flat-stemmed trifid in the mid-17th century. The functional approach was anticipated as early as 1904 by the brilliant Scottish designer, C. R. Mackintosh. The principle, however, was developed chiefly in Germany and Austria early in this century, with restrained designs based on 18th-century spoons.

During the 1930s, the lead was taken by Scandinavia, in a number of patterns so free of affectation that some are still in production. By 1944, the style had been established with the simple Thebe pattern, designed by Folke Arström for the Swedish firm of Gense, and made in stainless steel. Steel demands relatively unornamented designs which can be machine-made. Their low cost of production has undoubtedly accelerated the general acceptance of such modern patterns as the unadorned Symbol (illustrated). This type had appeared in Scandinavia by the late 1940s and in most other countries in the 1950s. It relies for its appeal on its subtle and refined shaping, emphasized in this case by the matt finish. Machine production which required the minimum angle between the bowl and stem soon produced designs in which the bowl is merely a scoop-like extension to a wide flat stem.

Functional styling was promoted throughout the world by numerous competitions, and in the 1950s and 1960s more designers of repute turned their hand to flatware than at any time before. Nevertheless, there was a reaction to the simple approach, exemplified in such spoons as the Studio pattern shown here.

Handles of wood and ivory, which had on the whole died out in the 19th century, reappeared on ordinary spoons by the 1930s, and nylon handles—usually given a matt surface—appeared in the 1950s, first in Scandinavia.

Left to right: Dessert spoon, furrow pattern, Sheffield 1955; designer, W.P. Belk, registered 1951; typical of English patterns produced c. 1950, and was also made in stainless steel; makers, Roberts and Belk. Tablespoon, studio pattern, stainless steel; designer, Gerald Benney; maker, Viners of Sheffield, from 1965; stamped STAINLESS STEEL/ STUDIO/VINERS OF SHEFFIELD ENGLAND; 8 inches. Tablespoon, Bistro pattern, stainless steel and rosewood; designer, Robert Welch, 1963; maker, Old Hall Tableware, Birmingham; stamped OLD HALL STAINLESS ENGLAND. Tablespoon, Sheffield 1965; designer and maker, Robert Welch. Tablespoon, symbol pattern, stainless steel; designer, David Mellor; maker, Walker and Hall, Sheffield; pattern received London Design Centre Award, 1962.

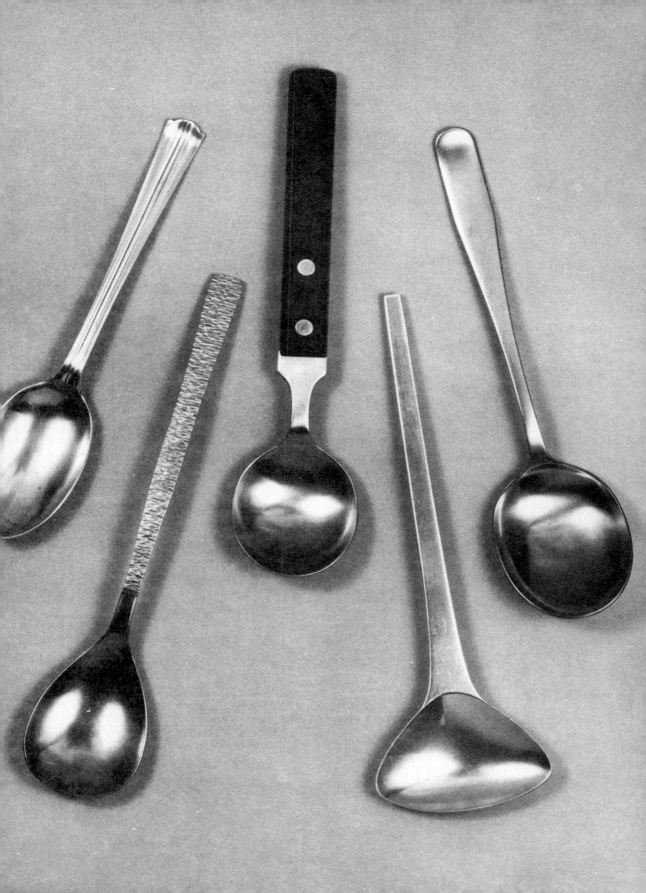

Bibliography

General and International

BURY, S. *Victorian Electroplate.* London and New York, 1971.

HARRIS, J. *The Price Guide to Antique Silver.* Woodbridge, 1969-70.

HOLLAND, J. 'A Treatise on the Progressive Improvement & Present State of the Manufactures in Metal.' *The Cabinet Cyclopedia of the Arts.* 3 vols. London, 1831-4.

HUGHES, G. *Modern Silver Throughout the World, 1880-1967.* London, 1967.

WARDLE, P. *Victorian Silver and Silver Plate.* London, 1963.

American

ANDREWS, W. *Architecture, Ambition and Americans.* New York, and London, 1955.

GIBB, G. S. *The Whitesmiths of Taunton: A History of Reed and Barton.* Cambridge, Mass., 1943.

GILES BROTHERS AND COMPANY. *Chicago Trade List and Jewelers' Reference Book.* Chicago, Ill., 1878.

MONTGOMERY, C. F. *A History of American Pewter.* New York and Washington, 1973.

New England Mercantile Union Business Directory. New York, 1849.

RAINWATER, D. and FELGER, D. H. *American Spoons Souvenir and Historical.* New Jersey, Pennsylvania, and Ontario, 1968.

RAINWATER, D. J. *Encyclopedia of American Silver Manufacturers.* New York, 1975.

Souvenir Spoons of America. Jewelers' Circular Publishing Company, 1891.

Technological Innovation and the Decorative Arts: Winterthur Conference Report 1973. ed. I.M.G. Quimby and P. E. Earl. Henry Francis du Pont Winterthur Museum: University Press of Virginia, 1974.

TURNER, N. D. *American Silver Flatware 1837-1910.* London and New York, 1972.

British and European

BENNET-CLARK, H. 'The Importance of Taste in Plate, Sheffield Plate Flatware', *Country Life* London, Feb. 1973, pp. 388-9.

BRADBURY, F. *History of Old Sheffield Plate.* Sheffield, 1912, reprinted 1968.

DELIEB, E. *Investing in Silver.* London and New York, 1967.

EMERY, J. *European Spoons before 1700.* Edinburgh, 1976.

HIMSWORTH, J. B. *The Story of Cutlery.* London, 1953.

PICKFORD, I. 'Flatware', *The Antique Finder* (London), vol. 14, No. 7, July 1975, pp. 9-13.

PINTO, E. H. *Treen and other Wooden Bygones.* London, 1969.

SNODIN, M. *English Silver Spoons.* London, 1974.

WHYTE, J. S. 'Scottish Georgian Silver Spoons', *The Antique Collector* (London) August 1969, pp. 163-167. 'Scottish Silver Teaspoons', *Scottish Art Review* (Glasgow), vol X, No. 4, 1969. 'Scottish Silver Tablespoons' *Scottish Art Review* (Glasgow), vol XI, No. 2, 1967.

Much material is contained in trade catalogues, mostly dating from after 1850. Catalogues exist for Christofle (Paris), James Dixon and Son (Sheffield), Elkington and Company (Birmingham), The Goldsmiths' and Silversmiths' Company (London), Francis Higgins and Son (London), Walker and Hall Limited (Sheffield) and others.

British and European Marks

FOTHERINGHAM, H. S. 'Scottish Provincial Silver', 'More Notes on Scottish Silver', 'Scottish Silver Curiosities'. *Antique Dealer and Collectors' Guide*, Aug. 1970, May 1972, Feb. 1975.

GRIMWADE, A. G. *London Goldsmiths 1697-1837, Their Marks and Lives.* London, 1976.

JACKSON, SIR CHARLES J. *English Goldsmiths and their Marks.* London, 1905. 2nd ed. 1921, reprinted 1949. Facsimile reprint, New York, 1964.

ROSENBERG, M. *Die Goldschmiede Merkzeichen,* 4 vols Frankfurt-am-Main and Berlin, 1922-1928.

TARDY, *Les Poinçons de Garantie Internationaux pour l'Argent.* 9th ed. Paris.

WYLER, S. B. *The Book of Sheffield Plate.* New York, 1949.

'Trade marks and Trade Names', *The National Association of Goldsmiths' Journal* (London), December 1930.

Picture acknowledgements

Page numbers given, those in italics refer to colour

The Henry Francis du Pont Winterthur Museum, Winterthur, Delaware: 13, 17, *23, 33, 35, 37, 45, 49, 59, 61, 71, 79.* Victoria & Albert Museum, London; F. Bechet de Balan; Private Collection: *15,* 43. Private collection: 19. The Henry Francis Du Pont Winterthur Museum, Winterthur, Delaware; Private collection: *21.* Victoria & Albert Museum, London; Hastings Museum & Art Gallery; Mr R. Chenciner: *25.* Victoria & Albert Museum, London; Private Collection: *27.* Victoria & Albert Museum, London; Francis J.C. Cooper: *29.* Collection of Kenneth & Gail Ames: 31, 73, 89, 93, 95, 97. Victoria & Albert Museum, London; M. McAleer, London; Mrs Jean Schofield; Private collection: 39. The Henry Francis du Pont Winterthur Museum Libraries, gift of Mr & Mrs Alfred E. Bissell: 41, 65, 69. Victoria & Albert Museum, London: 47, *63.* Victoria & Albert Museum, London; M. McAleer, London; Private Collection: 51. N. Bloom & Son, London: M. McAleer, London; Private Collection: *53.* Victoria & Albert Museum, London; M. McAleer, London; Harrowdine Bros. of Maidenhead; F. Bechet de Balan: 55. Victoria & Albert Museum, London; Sotheby's Belgravia; F. Bechet de Balan; Mrs Hugh Colman; Private Collection: 57. Victoria & Albert Museum, London; M. McAleer, London; Sotheby's Belgravia; Mr G.S. Sell: 67. Victoria & Albert Museum, London; M. McAleer, London; Sotheby's Belgravia; Private collection: *75.* Victoria & Albert Museum, London; M. McAleer, London; F. Bechet de Balan; Private collection: 77, *87.* Victoria & Albert Museum, London; M. McAleer, London; Sotheby's Belgravia; Harrowdine Bros. of Maidenhead; C.J. Shrubsole; Private collection: *83.* M. McAleer, London; C.J. Vander (Antiques) Ltd.; F. Bechet de Balan; Mrs Jean Schofield; Private collection: 85. Victoria & Albert Museum, London; M. McAleer, London; C.J. Vander (Antiques) Ltd.; Mrs Jean Schofield; Private collection: *91.* Victoria & Albert Museum, London; M. McAleer, London; Sotheby's Belgravia; Fine Arts Society, London; Haslam & Whiteway, London: *99.* Collection of Mr & Mrs Walter Day Mertz: 101. Collection of Mr & Mrs Donald L. Fennimore: *103.* Worshipful Company of Goldsmiths; M. McAleer, London; Mrs Jean Schofield; Private collection: 105. Worshipful Company of Goldsmiths: 107.

The following photographers were commissioned to take photographs for this book:
George J. Fistrovich: 13, 17, *21, 23, 33, 35, 37, 45, 49, 59, 61, 71, 79, 103.*
A.C. Cooper Limited, London: *15,* 19, *25, 27, 29,* 39, 43, 47, 51, *53,* 55, 57, *63, 67, 75,* 77, 81, *83,* 85, *87, 91, 99.*
Wayne B. Gibson: 31, 41, 65, 69, 73, 89, 93, 95, 97, 101.
Peter Parkinson: 105, 107.

Index